The
Insurance
Agent's Guide
to TELEPHONE
PROSPECTING

MONEY-MAKING POWER STRATEGIES
FROM A TOP TELEPROSPECTOR

LOU ELLEN DAVIS

Financial Sourcebooks
A Division of Sourcebooks, Inc.
P.O. Box 313 ▪ Naperville, Illinois 60566
(708) 961-2161 ▪ Fax (708) 961-2168

Library of Congress Cataloging-in-Publication Data

Davis, Lou Ellen,
    Tele-prospecting : warming up the cold call to increase your
income / Lou Ellen Davis.
        p. cm.
    Includes index.
    ISBN 0-13-140252-8
    1. Telemarketing. 2. Insurance—Agents. I. Title.
HF5415.1265.D38   1992
658.8'4—dc20   92-2949
                                                                      CIP

This publication is designed to provide accurate and authoritative
information in regard to the subject matter covered. It is sold with the
understanding that the publisher is not engaged in rendering legal,
accounting, or other professional service. If legal advice or other expert
assistance is required, the services of a competent professional person should
be sought.

From a Declaration of Principles Jointly Adopted by a Committee of the
American Bar Association and a Committee of Publishers and Associations

Printed in the United States of America

10 9 8 7 6 5 4 3 2 1

ISBN 0-13-140252-8

New York Institute of Finance
Simon & Schuster
A Paramount Communications Company

PREFACE

Teleprospecting (in any business) is a process in which salespeople or others whom they have hired pick up the *telephone* and call *prospects* who are complete strangers, to set up *appointments* through which, it is hoped, the salespeople will eventually sell their product. As used in this book, tele*marketing* is a similar process, except that the goal is not to set up appointments. Rather, it is to close a sale over the phone, to directly *market* by *tele*phone a product.

   Telephone cold calling is a generic term encompassing both categories.

   Probably if you have been in the life and health (L&H) end of the insurance business for more than a year or so—and *possibly* if you specialize in property and casualty (P&C)—you are already familiar with insurance teleprospecting.

   If you are an insurance professional so turned off by your teleprospecting experiences that you never want to hear or see anything else even remotely connected with the topic, grit your teeth if you must, but keep reading!

   Or perhaps you have no particular feelings on the subject. Your bottom line is: You're okay without it. If your area of specialization is L&H, this may mean you're relatively new in the business, still riding high on referrals *which have not yet been exhausted,* as a source of new clients.

But L&H referrals very often run dry, usually within the first two years, *which is the time frame during which approximately one-half of all new insurance salespeople leave the business*!

Or perhaps your area is P&C; referrals and/or walk-ins and/or responses to ads keep you so busy, the idea of actively pursuing more business—especially by any means as tedious and time consuming as telephone cold calling—strikes you as rather silly.

If your area is P&C, indeed it may strike *you* as silly, *but don't count on your chief competitors feeling the same way.*

"We steal clients every day," states Adam Seid, co-owner of Randall Marc Marketing, a Los Angeles–based insurance teleprospecting firm which, among other services, calls P&C policyholders throughout the country, setting up sales appointments for local insurance salespeople all seeking to underbid and/or out-class-on-service current carriers the instant a policy comes up for renewal.

In addition, today throughout America, ever-increasing numbers of L&H professionals are recognizing that one of the until recently most neglected and very best ways to solidly connect with potential L&H clients is to teleprospect them and make an *appointment* to sell a relatively minor personal P&C product!

But others, in addition to individual insurance salespeople, can benefit from these pages.

Because even large groups are comprised of individuals, managers of teleprospecting in-house or outside service operations who implement what is recommended in these pages on improving individual performance will quantifiably improve their overall results.

Especially if you manage a multiservice outside operation, it is probably apparent to you that insurance appointments are generally considerably more difficult to obtain than sales appointments for other products. This book can help you to improve results for your insurance clients.

If you are an executive at any level in any banking or other financial institution, and are responsible for telephone-based insurance sales as a profit center within the larger structure, this book will prove invaluable to your success.

If you are a freelance telephone solicitor—one of the many thousands who turn to whatever cold calling may be available when they need a few extra dollars—these pages can help you to succeed in one of the toughest and best paying specialties in the country!

Although the material here focuses on *insurance* cold calling, much of it is universal and therefore applicable to a far broader range of products. If you are not in the insurance business and think you've already read everything anyone could possibly write about telephone prospecting in your particular product or service area, if you pick up this book, you will probably be surprised and delighted by how much new material you will discover.

However, whatever your business and whether your goal is to initiate a successful telephone prospecting operation, to enhance an existing one, or merely in the name of self-defense, to stay on top of what your competition is *probably* already doing in this area, be prepared not only to read this book, but to keep it handy as an ongoing reference source.

ACKNOWLEDGMENTS

The following is a professional courtesy acknowledgment of *some* of the people who contributed to this book, but it is also deeply personal. Because most of the interviews were conducted by phone, I now feel as though I have many new friends I've never met. I was particularly touched by those who so freely offered their best, often personally developed sales tools for a book which they knew would be read by other salespeople, tools offered with a generosity of spirit completely transcending competitive self-interest.

I especially thank my New York Institute of Finance editor, Sheck Cho, largely for the pleasure of working with him, but also for his excellent idea to expand the geographical base far beyond what I had originally proposed; and Price Gaines, CLU, RHU, a leading insurance industry professional editor and writer for over 30 years, for his initial faith in the overall project, followed by his final, detailed page-by-page recommendations.

People outside the industry are also included, for example, Sondra Watson, a former insurance industry telephone cold caller who now leads stress-reduction-through-humor workshops and talks of the importance of "having fun with what you're doing" in reducing cold-calling stress, and my former cousin-in-law Col. Walter E. Price, U.S. Army Ret., who tried so hard to find an appropriate interview subject for me in the state of Oklahama (I'm sure they're there, but eventually both of us gave up!).

And I gratefully acknowledge my friend John McDowell for his ever-patient moral support.

Still, the list is incomplete because to encompass everyone who contributed through the years would be prohibitive in length. But to those not included, I add the same "thank you!" offered to those whose names appear below.

The list is in alphabetical order, according to state.

Bud Davidson, Dean S. Davidson Insurance Agency; Joni Fairbrother, Independent Insurance Agents & Brokers of Arizona (Arizona). Randall Marc and Adam Seid, Randall Marc Marketing; Jack Nordhaus, vice president, Information Services, Insurance Marketing and Information Services; Rayda Roundy and Barbara Schiefer, of George Porter's El Camino Insurance Agency (California).

Randy Crawford (Colorado). Ned Mann, managing editor, Life Insurance Marketing Research Association (Connecticut). Karen Placek, president, Telephone Marketing Promotions, Inc. (Florida). Walter V. Worsham III, CLU, ChFC, The Worsham Organization (Georgia). Ned Burns and John Linley, MDS Insurance; L. Dwayne Query, Query Insurance Agency; Harry Woolen (Illinois).

Charlene Jacobsen, manager, Breda Telemarketing (Iowa). Shari Halloran; Toshiko N. Molden, executive secretary, Topeka Association of Life Underwriters (Kansas). Irving H. Shaw, CLU, ChFC, RHU, LUTCF, chief executive officer, Shaw American Companies (Kentucky). Antoinette Hondroulis (Louisiana). Craig Beachaw, LIC (Michigan). Mike Axton; Dorothy Scott (Mississippi). David P. Davis, director of telemarketing, Metro Management Associates (New Jersey).

Kristine Bernhardt, account executive, Business Communications, Metropolitan Life Insurance Company; Charlotte G. Crandall, association executive, Syracuse Association of Life Underwriters; Keith Dawson, writer, *Inbound / Outbound Magazine*; Joe Foster and Mark Rubin, Massachusetts Mutual; Carl Gerson, CLU, CPCU, ChFC, executive vice president, Property and Life Planners; Sigrid Hanser-Ifrah, CM Alliance; Carol Kitrosser, Perlow Financial Group; George Lehmuller; Ed Lennon, sales manager, Luis Tejada Prudential Agency; Al Levine; Emmanuel Levy, editor, *Insurance Advocate*; Susan Rodetes; Sondra Watson; David Wexler (New York).

Larry Houser; Clair Thompson, Vaaler Insurance (North Dakota). Laurie Prevett, RHU, Equity Brokerage, Inc. (North Carolina). Price Gaines, CLU, RHU (Ohio). Col. Walter E. Price, U.S. Army Ret. (Oklahoma). Bob Beswick, CLU, Pacific Mutual (Oregon).

Quinter G. Colebank, CLU, executive vice president, Pittsburgh Life Underwriters Association; Joe Olesky, Metropolitan Life Insurance (Pennsylvania). Thomas Masi, LUTCS, The Shirley Merrill Agency (South Carolina). Suzanna Edwards; William J. Grimes (Texas). Rebecca Paquette, executive director, Independent Insurance Agents of Vermont, Inc.; Paul Poulos, Poulos Insurance, Inc. (Vermont). Karen Fruchtl, Spencer-Kinney; Judy Peterson and Tom Taylor, Jr., CPCU, Tom Taylor Insurance Brokers, Inc. (Washington). Carol Ferrante, director of association services, General Agents and Managers Association; Jay Morris, Public Relations, The National Association of Life Underwriters (Washington, D.C.). Jeannine Opsal, executive director, Independent Insurance Agents of Wyoming (Wyoming).

I also thank "Chris," the organization librarian who was so helpful, but did not want to be identified because she was afraid she would consequently receive more calls for help than she could handle!

CONTENTS

GLOSSARY

In putting together this material, I discovered certain voids in industry terminology. Because the terminology either does not exist or exists confusingly with no universally accepted meanings for the same words, much of what I've used is arbitrary but carefully chosen to meet the need for consistency and clarity in this book.

If occasionally I seem to be defining the obvious, please be patient. Many experts in one area are surprisingly unfamiliar with *related* information in other areas. In these pages, to help maximize teleprospecting return on investment, certain co-marketing options are explored, thus requiring an understanding of information quite obvious to some but relatively unfamiliar to others.

Throughout, as new terms are introduced in the text, they are defined (and often redefined, to minimize the disruption of having to refer back), which means *there is no need to put any particular effort into learning this glossary; it is hoped that you will absorb most of it quite naturally as you go along.*

However, if you do run into words or phrases you've forgotten, and want to double-check quickly, the definitions are presented here.

AGENT—although in some states, there are technical (and sometimes legal) distinctions between an AGENT and a *broker*, common industry usage generally lumps both together under AGENT. Therefore, in the interests of keeping it both simple and consistent, in this book, an AGENT is anyone licensed to sell insurance. The terms AGENT, SALESPERSON, and PRODUCER are synonymous.

COLD CALLING—although in common industry usage, this *can* mean unexpectedly dropping in on a potential client in person; unless otherwise specified, *in this book* it refers to *telephoning* a stranger (not a present client) for the purpose of either directly selling an insurance product over the phone (TELE*MARKETING*) or arranging an *appointment* to sell a product (TELE*PROSPECTING*).

EX-DATE—see X-DATE

INDEPENDENT CALLERS (or, simply, Independents)—sharp, usually well-paid, often very sophisticated OUTSIDE CALLERS who generally work pretty much on their own, with minimal supervision, often preparing their own material.

IN-HOUSE OPERATIONS—on-premises TELEPROSPECTING or TELEMARKETING operations within individual agencies or insurance companies or other financial institutions sponsoring the sale of insurance products.

LEAD PRODUCT—primary, usually catchy product used in TELEMARKETING or TELEPROSPECTING to hook the listener's attention quickly.

L&H—life & health insurance

MONKEYS-WITH-A-SCRIPT—(I didn't create it!) a commonly used, albeit unkind, synonym for REGIMENTED CALLERS.

OUTSIDE CALLERS—TELEPROSPECTORS arranging telephone COLD-CALL sales appointments for anyone other than himself or herself (as opposed to a salesperson setting up his or her own appointments).

OUTSIDE OPERATIONS—opposite of IN-HOUSE OPERATIONS, synonymous with OUTSIDE ORGANIZATIONS and SERVICE FIRMS.

OUTSIDE ORGANIZATIONS—synonymous with OUTSIDE OPERATIONS and SERVICE FIRMS.

P&C—property & casualty insurance

PITCH—the material presented to a telephone prospect, sometimes written out, sometimes ad-libbed, often a combination of both. *This is largely a geographical term.* To some, it suggests (offensively) a carnival product, but to others, any book without it would seem seriously incomplete. Therefore, with respect for those accustomed to using PITCH, it is used throughout this book, but with equal respect for those who are unhappy with it, TELEPHONE PRESENTATION is also used. The two terms are synonymous.

PRESENTATION—short for TELEPHONE PRESENTATION, synonymous with PITCH. See PITCH.

PRODUCER—synonymous with SALESPERSON and AGENT (defined under AGENT).

PROSPECT—within the industry, common use of this word is unclear. Sometimes it means anyone who might possibly buy insurance. At other times, it suggests screening past the "suspect" stage into a higher degree of likelihood. As used in this book, the first definition applies: a PROSPECT is anyone approached as a potential client.

REGIMENTED CALLERS—OUTSIDE CALLERS working under close supervision, usually in groups, for comparatively little money, with material prepared by others.

SALESPERSON—synonymous with AGENT and PRODUCER, defined under AGENT.

SERVICE FIRMS—service operations not based in the insurance salesperson's premises, managed by people who are generally not insurance salespeople, offering TELEMARKETING or TELEPROSPECTING services to insurance salespeople who want sales/appointments through this process, but choose not to participate directly in or manage it themselves.

SCRIPT—a strict guide on what to say, designed to be read word for word by telephone cold callers.

SCRIPTED CALLS (or CALLERS)—calls in which (or by whom) a SCRIPT is strictly followed.

TELEMARKETING—using the *tele*phone to *market* directly a specific insurance *product*; actually to close a sale *initiated by the caller*, over the phone (this does *not* apply when the buyer has initiated contact with the seller, as is often the case in property & casualty telephone sales).

TELEPHONE PRESENTATION—synonymous with PRESEN-TATION and PITCH. See PITCH.

TELEPROSPECTING—using the *tele*phone to call *prospects* who are complete strangers, to set up face-to-face appointments through which, it is hoped, that salespeople will eventually sell insurance. TELEPROSPECTING can be done *either by OUTSIDE CALLERS or by AGENTS setting their own appointments*.

WARM CALLING—following up, by telephone, on a referral or with someone you've at least met.

X-DATE—sometimes also seen in industry publications as "EX-DATE." The two are synonymous. To maintain consistency in this book, "X-DATE" has been arbitrarily selected. An X-DATE is the date on which a present policy expires if not renewed, most commonly (although not exclusively) used in property & casualty insurance TELEPROSPECTING.

X-DATE CALLING—calling policyholders who are clients of competitors, for the specific purpose of learning when their present coverage expires, to facilitate additional contact during the critical period when the decision on whether or not to renew with their present carrier will be made.

INTRODUCTION

SOUND: TELEPHONE R-I-N-G-S

PROSPECT: Hello?

CALLER: Hi. I sell insurance. Wanna buy some?

PROSPECT: Insurance? Absolutely! I'm so glad you called! How much will you sell me?

CALLER: Hey—how much can you pay for?

PROSPECT: I'll mortgage my house; sell my dog! When can we meet? Your convenience.

CALLER: Well, I'm afraid it'll be awhile before I can fit you in. People like us who call complete strangers like you to sell them insurance are very much in demand, you know.

Wasn't that nice? Now let's go back to reality.

Teleprospecting—the process of *prospecting* by *telephone,* which boils down to calling complete strangers for sales appointments—is a major marketing tool used in two distinct product categories. The first category is insurance; the second is everything else.

Insurance product categories also are commonly divided by twos: for openers, life & health (L&H), then property & casualty (P&C).

Still moving along two by two, both P&C and L&H further break down into *personal and/or family* and *commercial*. Techniques to improve telephone cold-calling success—sometimes dramatically—in all these categories will be explored in this book.

The assumption that if you can make it in New York, you can make it anywhere is not necessarily true when it comes to insurance cold calling. Some of the assertiveness essential to success in large, fast-moving cities like New York can translate into obnoxious overkill elsewhere, while some of what works well elsewhere would evoke only speed-of-light hang-ups in New York. With respect for this, among numerous other geographically based differences, people from other states who have contributed cold-calling experiences to these pages are identified by state.

Throughout, I've pretty much substituted *teleprospecting* for *telemarketing*, because the word "teleprospecting" seems more finely tuned to most insurance industry telephone cold calling. Although sometimes insurance products are sold directly over the phone—*marketed* by *tele*phone, or "telemarketed"—most insurance industry telephone cold calls are *prospecting* calls, and they are *tele*phone calls as opposed simply to arriving unannounced at the prospect's home or place of business. Through teleprospecting, a salesperson hopes to *make appointments* with *prospective* clients, appointments through which eventually insurance will be sold. *But the "product" which is directly "sold" in most successful teleprospecting calls is not insurance; it is appointments.*

Although recommendations to improve results in direct selling of insurance products by phone are included, the primary focus of this book is on securing appointments.

Teleprospecting is far more widely used in P&C sales than a lot of insurance professionals who don't use it realize, but the effort is rarely as organized or as intensive as in the L&H

arena. In P&C, often referrals and walk-in business, in conjunction with competitive pricing and superior service, are more than sufficient to keep an agency prosperous, *although this is changing.* Today, fixed costs are rising, in accord with other inflationary factors, but also, more and more major P&C insurance carriers are passing a higher percentage of *their* costs on to the P&C agents. Consequently, a more focused marketing effort geared to sustained *growth* is becoming necessary to sustain *present* profitability. However, at the moment this is still more a direction than a deluge in the P&C domain; many operations have not *yet* really thought it through.

In sharp contrast, L&H has *always* required *aggressive* ongoing marketing, with teleprospecting a primary tool. This is why when "teleprospecting" is used throughout this book, unless otherwise specified, the products it refers to are in the L&H category.

In L&H, mastering this skill—the fine art of picking up a phone and convincing complete strangers that it would be worth their time to meet with you—is often the deciding factor on whether you will go on to make an excellent living or whether you will, instead, become simply another statistic in the legions of drop-outs, those who, often after auspicious beginnings, within the first two or three years simply give up and walk away.

Nothing here is intended to suggest that most full-time L&H salespeople could make a living with no resource other than cold calling to carry them from sale to sale. With the quantity of effort that goes into securing even one appointment—in both L&H and in P&C teleprospecting, in conjunction with the number of appointments which turn out to be a waste of time—the *immediate* ratio on effort to income is rarely encouraging.

However, the key word is *immediate. Longer range,* even a few new clients—clients you would never have acquired without teleprospecting—can not only enhance your morale and income over many years with repeat and additional business, but often more important, *these clients enlarge your collective referral base.*

Granted, insurance industry teleprospecting is the second toughest telephone soliciting job in the world (let those with compulsively contradictory natures argue over what's first). However, this does not mean you cannot go for it and succeed. Most insurance industry teleprospectors—whether they are licensed insurance agents or simply individuals who make appointments for the agents—*are not functioning at anywhere near their potential.* The reasons for this will be explored in greater detail in the following pages, but worth special mention here is the fact that much of the problem stems from historically entrenched antiquated training programs within the insurance industry as a whole.

If you are feeling discouraged or angry over your present results, or, instead, if you've made peace with them but still would like to improve substantially (possibly even double, or better!) your overall teleprospecting return on investment, this book can be one of the most important you'll ever read.

Although managers and outside telemarketers can definitely benefit from this material, it is primarily geared to individual salespeople.

If you are an individual insurance agent, it will help you to make *informed* choices, across the board, in planning your personal teleprospecting campaigns. *Who should you be calling, when, with what door-opener products, and once you have a prospect on the phone, what should you say?*

And what is your overall plan on simply making enough money to live? Are you pursuing a balance between more difficult but also more lucrative sales and bread-and-butter shorter-term projects?

Have you analyzed backup support considerations, for example, when is it productive to send information or confirmation letters in conjunction with your telephone campaign and when is anything in this vein a waste of time and money?

When you do send out material, is it what it ought to be?

You will also find *emotional* support to help you deal with call resistance, rejection, discouragement, and burnout. Some will come from other professionals who have experienced and worked through these issues; much is based in my own experience.

If you decide to hire outsiders, this book will help you to locate, to train *properly*, and to communicate *effectively* with them.

You will also find help in establishing realistic standards against which to measure their performance.

This book will help you to *get organized*, to minimize, simplify, and clarify clerical support; for example, are you or your teleprospector spending more time writing up the results of each call than calling? How much information do you *really* need—and what's the quickest way to record it?

We'll discuss how to design and most effectively implement pitches, also referred to as telephone presentations. According to Adam Seid, co-owner of the Los Angeles–based insurance teleprospecting service firm mentioned in the preface, "The trick is not to sound like a telemarketer."

Sometimes, it's *one* "trick," but only one. By the time you finish these pages, you'll have picked up quite a few!

For over 25 years, off and on, I have worked as a telephone cold caller, primarily in the insurance industry, at one time or another dealing directly with every issue covered in this book. It started when my ex-husband, at that time my husband, was a young agent who hated teleprospecting. I was an actress with a trained speaking voice, also beginning to make money as a freelance writer; in short, I was an unusually good communicator with flexible hours.

For these reasons, among others, one day he asked me to come into his office to see whether I might be better at cold calling than he was. To avoid the appearance of a mom and pop operation, I used a different last name—and two of the people I called, not realizing the depth of my connection with my "employer," tried to hire me away from him to cold call for *their* businesses!

A lot of what I did that first day was intuitive; some was excellent, but some could have been much better. The right training, I have subsequently learned, always enhances—works with—intuition, although neither training nor intuition is ever a substitute for the other.

Today, as a consultant and trainer, I work a lot with external know-how, but throughout this book, you'll also find a careful interweaving of the emotional tools necessary to withstand the extraordinary internal pressures of cold calling.

The fact that you're looking at this book suggests that either you are seriously considering teleprospecting or that you have already tried it, but think—or hope—your results could be improved.

Probably—you're right!

CHAPTER 1

Insurance Industry Teleprospecting: What It Is, and What You Can Do About It!

INSURANCE COLD CALLING VERSUS EVERYTHING ELSE

Insurance is different. If you've done telephone cold calling in other fields or studied generic techniques and then tried to apply those techniques to insurance, you already know that insurance is unlike any other product out there.

Or perhaps you don't do your own calling; instead, you hire others. But whether you do it yourself or hire others, if you're new to the process, probably you're disappointed with your overall results. If you've been around awhile, more likely you're no longer disappointed, but this is because you've lowered your expectations—drastically!

"TELEPROSPECTING" DEFINED

"Teleprospecting" is *prospecting* by *tele*phone. The word seems particularly well suited to insurance telephone cold calling because although sometimes tangible insurance *products* are *marketed* by *tele*phone—*telemarketed*—in most cases, a successful tele*prospecting* call ends with nothing "sold" except an appointment. The *prospect*—not yet a customer—has agreed to meet with you. Through subsequent face-to-face contact, eventually some of these prospects will indeed become customers.

SELLING INSURANCE PRODUCTS BY PHONE

Although Chapter 4 looks at *telemarketing—tele*phone direct *market*ing of tangible products—in L&H, usually the scale of these operations influences their form and functioning in ways which set them very much apart from most tele*prospecting* operations. P&C agents also sometimes sell directly over the phone, but with most P&C phone sales, the agent did not cold call to find the client; instead, the client found the agent, which makes the process very different indeed from *either* teleprospecting *or* telemarketing.

WIDE RANGE ON VARIETY AND QUALITY OF TELEPROSPECTED APPOINTMENTS

In teleprospecting, no matter how well you construct and execute your campaign, you are dealing with far more variables and usually considerably less hard data than when you connect with someone either through a referral or through carrying business cards with you wherever you go, and going a lot of places where you will meet a lot of people; teleprospecting is *cold* calling.

Consequently, the appointments you net will encompass a far broader range than you are probably used to on *quality* and *predictability*.

However, most salespeople who teleprospect do so because the number of clients available to them through other sources is inadequate, and of the available alternatives, teleprospecting seems the most promising.

And it *is* promising—but, at times, also outrageously frustrating! In fact, some cold calls make you wonder why you ever bothered to pick up the phone, while others delight you with the answer.

It is the purpose of this book to maximize your success in connecting with prospects who will delight you.

JUSTIFYING YOUR TELEPROSPECTING COST

When prospects with whom you have set appointments through teleprospecting become customers, *they lay the groundwork for repeat and add-on business, while also enhancing your collective client base for future referrals.* This continuing personal relationship is one of many elements which sets most teleprospecting-based sales apart from most telemarketing sales. It is also a major factor in keeping teleprospecting cost effective for individual agents. If you had to rely on teleprospecting as your sole basis for leads in every sale, you would quickly discover that in terms of either your time or time bought from someone you've hired, it is far too expensive. But as a *resource to renew and revitalize your overall business momentum continually,* mastering teleprospecting can easily become one of the most important career investments you'll ever make!

L&H TELEPROSPECTING

If your area of specialization is L&H, and you've been in it for any length of time, you know that eventually the original wells that nourished you by providing clients run dry. The friends and relatives you sold to when you entered the business—and everyone they referred you to—eventually are no longer an adequate source of new business.

At this point, teleprospecting *is frequently a make-or-break factor on whether you will remain in the insurance business*. Most newcomers last only two years—or less!

P&C TELEPROSPECTING

However, perhaps your area of specialization is P&C. The majority of the P&C salespeople interviewed for this book do not teleprospect, but many do and are quite successful at it, although usually their cold-calling operations are on a smaller scale than in L&H. Most industry teleprospecting is in L&H, usually by callers who know very little about P&C. With few exceptions (Aetna, Allstate, and Travelers), this simply reflects the financial structure of the industry; P&C and L&H are separate with, among other distinctions, a very different commission structure. To stay afloat in L&H, an agent must pursue heavy ongoing new production, while P&C success is based far more often on retaining present clients through ongoing superior service, which very much accounts for why teleprospecting in the L&H area is, collectively, so much heavier than in P&C.

DIFFERENCES BETWEEN P&C AND L&H GENERAL MARKETING APPROACHES

Quantity of teleprospecting is not the only area in which marketing approaches between L&H and P&C differ. It is an industry axiom that P&C is *purchased*, while life insurance is *sold*. Although referrals from present clients are always a critically important new business source in either area, far more P&C than L&H offices operate from storefronts, to draw walk-in business, and you might want to note how many more *display* ads you will find in your local Yellow Pages for P&C insurance than for L&H. Among smaller operations, usually *personal* P&C, a common philosophy is, *we'll let our clients find us; if we had to go out and find them, none of us would have time to make a living.*

Ideally, however, not even advertising or storefront offices are necessary. Instead, old clients remain steadfast while now referrals multiply like rabbits, over the years.

P&C NEW BUSINESS ALL THROUGH REFERRALS

Carl Gerson, CLU, CPCU, ChFC, a second-generation salesman in the P&C business started by his father, Barry, until very recently, epitomized the ideal. The office takes up all of the fourth floor in a Manhattan relatively low-overhead area, with nothing to tell a passerby it's there except the building directory listing. Although *most* of the company's business is still through referrals by present clients, like many others specializing in P&C, Carl is now actively seeking expansion to protect his present profit margin in the face of rising costs and is using an outside teleprospecting firm (Randall Marc Marketing, in California) to generate new leads. Carl's company, Property and Life Planners, is relatively elite; many individual clients pay five-figure annual premiums.

In answering why he did *not* pursue new leads through any channel other than referrals until recently, Carl presents a vivid picture contrasting P&C business in general with the far more aggressive marketing environment common to L&H. Remember, P&C renewals include a higher commission percentage than L&H. Thus, the *time* for P&C service is more available; time which is necessary because P&C requires more.

"Something's always changing," Carl explains. "The size and consequent insurance needs of a business grow larger or smaller, or simply change. Something of value is damaged or stolen. Someone whose car insurance we handle has an accident. All this takes time. We barely have time to service the clients we already have and to follow up on new business referrals. This is why the *active* expansion we're pursuing now means we'll need to take on more producers to handle it."

COLD AND "WARM" CALLING PROMOTE P&C NEW BUSINESS

In Tacoma, Washington, Tom Taylor, Jr., CPCU, has been selling insurance for 26 years. He has two offices, both handling predominantly P&C, with combined premiums in excess of $5 million a year. Tom feels he has "enough" business but is *open* to expansion, although "in a controlled way. We generate an X-date list," he explains. An "X-date" is the date on which a present policy will expire if not renewed. "Then we have someone spend an hour or so on the phone every day, to set up appointments 30 to 60 days before the policies are up for renewal." This, virtually all industry professionals believe, is the critical time period during which an even slightly dissatisfied client is most likely to consider seriously proposals from competitors.

However, the list is "generated" through personal contacts, not cold calling. "We collect X-dates all the time when we talk to anybody about anything. The data goes into the computer.

"We also have a 'life man' (life insurance sales-man)," he adds, but in proportion to the agency's P&C sales, L&H is negligible.

However, Tom does not *cold* call; more appropriately, the telephone soliciting done in his office would have to be classified as, at minimum, lukewarm.

Notwithstanding, in New Orleans, independent telemarketer Antoinette Hondroulis has done P&C cold calling quite successfully from the Yellow Pages on an industry-by-industry basis.

Karen Placek, president of Telephone Marketing Promotions Inc., an insurance teleprospecting service firm with two offices in Florida and another in Illinois, feels very strongly that P&C is the *only* insurance area in which teleprospecting for personal lines insurance makes sense; as a *commercial* lines door-opener, she uses group health.

"Life insurance cold calling equals burnout," she says. "We don't do that to our telemarketers. We want them to succeed, to feel good about what they're doing. So many insurance salespeople go for life and disability. They think, 'it only takes one good one.' What they don't understand is that whether you're pursuing personal or commercial line big sales, the little ones can *become* big."

"HYBRID" MARKETING—P&C "DOOR-OPENERS" FOR LIFE SALES

In Queens, New York, Ed Lennon, sales manager of the Luis Tejada Rego Park Prudential agency validates much of Karen's philosophy. In his early thirties with a six-figure income, Ed, like Barry Gerson, works on an upper floor in an office building and does not advertise. But the primary door-opener for Ed's *life* sales is *P&C cold calling*!

None of Ed's business is commercial; it's all personal, and competitors in Ed's territory who hope to retain their walk-in or secured-through-advertising personal P&C clients would be well advised not to take any pending renewals for granted. "I've got 15 salespeople here," says Ed. "If I had to wait for customers to call or walk in off the street, I'd be out of business.

"Usually, we call and tell people we can *probably* save them money on their car insurance."

According to Joni Fairbrother who teaches cold calling in Phoenix under the auspices of the Independent Insurance Agents and Brokers of Arizona, the single best P&C door-opener is, indeed, auto insurance.

However, because not everyone owns a car, alternatives are necessary. Alternative products tend to be less homogeneous, more often determined by needs intrinsic to a particular area. Often these requirements are relatively constant, but sometimes focusing on *changing* P&C needs can be especially effective.

"*With so many buildings in the neighborhood going co-op*, sometimes we pursue co-op insurance," Ed continues. "No, you can't make a living telemarketing for appointments to sell only co-op or car insurance, but once you're in and you've built credibility, very often you'll find you're handling all their insurance needs. Actually only 10 percent of the agency's total business is P&C. Another 5 percent is mutual funds, 5 percent is health, 5 percent is annuities—*and the rest is life.*"

Like others who do *any* P&C, Ed emphasizes service. "If we don't come through on the service, just as we took business away from someone else, someone else will take it away from us."

BIG MARKET FOR P&C X-DATES

A primary asset in the process of "stealing" P&C clients is knowing when their present policies expire. Obtaining these expiration dates by telephone, or "X-date calling" as it is more commonly referred to, has become its own area of specialization. Based in California, Randall Marc Marketing sets up appointments for insurance agents throughout the country, but also collects X-dates in commercial P&C and life and disability. In Florida and Illinois, Karen Placek's teleprospecting firm, Telephone Marketing Promotions, Inc., also calls nationally, collecting X-dates in both personal and commercial lines.

"The blood of your agency is your X-date file," she states without reservation.

SUCCEEDING WITH L&H-ONLY TELEPROSPECTING

Although small-scale P&C products are often sadly neglected door-openers for more lucrative L&H sales, not everyone agrees that L&H teleprospecting *necessarily* equals burnout. Many successful L&H teleprospectors believe the problem is not at all intrinsic to all L&H products per se; rather it is in the *particular product being offered, the prospects to whom it is being offered, and in the teleprospector's presentation.* Far too many otherwise sharp salespeople do not realize that *not every income group or profession lends itself to a teleprospecting approach.*

Incorporating these realities into your initial planning can make all the difference on whether you will succeed or fail with this very powerful marketing tool. Much more on this will be presented in subsequent chapters.

L&H PRIMARY FOCUS OF THESE PAGES

Because L&H dominates insurance telephone soliciting so powerfully (even though P&C is definitely expanding!), from this point on, unless otherwise specified, when "insurance" is mentioned it refers to L&H.

POOR OVERALL TELEPROSPECTING TRAINING

Unfortunately—ironically—the teleprospecting training offered by virtually all insurance companies leaves much to be desired; ironic because the industry as a whole spends astronomical sums on training to keep its salespeople in state-of-the-art readiness to sell state-of-the-art products.

Yet some of the scripts used today read as though they hadn't been updated in generations. "Good morning, Mr. Prospect. How are you?" Generations ago, this was okay. *Even in small towns, the pace was slower than today.* People rode on trains instead of planes, and nobody had ever heard of a microwave. If you took an extra few seconds to get to the point, that was fine. *Nor were there anywhere near as many cold callers as there are today.* One industry source projects that by the end of this decade, there will be somewhere in excess of *14 million* telemarketers in this country selling by telephone any and everything imaginable. And that number encompasses human beings only; it makes no allowance for the *machines* that also cold call!

THE ASTERISK LAWS

The "asterisk laws," already adopted in several states, reflect the number of people who feel oversolicited by telephone. In essence, everyone within the state who is unwilling to receive such calls (charitable organizations are sometimes excluded from the restriction) indicates this by placing an asterisk beside his or her name in the phone directory.

WHY "MR. PROSPECT" IS ANNOYED BY YOUR PITCH

But even if Mr. Prospect neglected to exercise this option, which probably was not available to him anyway since most states do not have asterisk laws, the truth is, when your call comes in, far more often than not he's busy, he's annoyed, your call is at least the third cold call he's received that day—even if it's only 9:15 A.M.—and the last thing he has any interest in is discussing his health with a total stranger, *particularly* one who probably wants to sell him something. Also remember, all this is before he even knows that your product is insurance. And this is only the *beginning* of the presentation; we haven't even gotten to the second sentence.

POOR TRAINING IN WORKING WITH INDEPENDENT TELEPROSPECTORS

Nor is the training offered to insurance salespeople on how to *work with* outside callers (anyone other than an agent cold calling to make appointments for the agent) any better. Far too often resentments pile up on both sides, usually as a result of communication problems which easily could have been avoided.

In addition, if you hire more than one outsider, or if you share the same outsider with other producers, how do you define essential boundaries? Who calls for whom, in what areas, and when? And how is this to be determined?

An especially successful two-person teleprospecting operation in a medium-sized West Coast agency fell apart on this issue with such passion, the operation was never reinstituted. The manager was also a producer—and took all the good appointments for himself. Also, the administrative support was so bad, a number of other appointments weren't even kept, which upset the teleprospectors as much as the other producers had been upset by the manager skimming the cream. Eventually, the teleprospectors—and two agents—left.

None of this was at all necessary.

SETTING APPOINTMENTS VERSUS SELLING INSURANCE

Even well-paid extraordinary teleprospectors cannot come through for you at anywhere near their maximum potential without your understanding and support. *Very* few insurance professionals really comprehend the difference between selling *appointments* as opposed to selling insurance. They are very different products, *requiring very different selling skills.* When you sit down with an appointment, presumably you have the prospect's attention and at least some measure of interest in your product. But when you cold call, you constitute an uninvited and frequently *very* annoying interruption.

It's often been said that in an insurance cold call, you have only 30 seconds to hook your prospect's interest. Perhaps in parts of the country where the pace of life is relatively slow, this is true. However, in large cosmopolitan oversolicited cities like Phoenix, Los Angeles, and New York, usually it's more like 10!

IT'S *NOT* "ALL NUMBERS"

Another almost universal misconception is the idea that "It's all numbers. Make enough calls; you'll sell some insurance." Indeed you will—but how many calls *are* "enough"?

Reality is, it's *not* "all numbers." Although certainly numbers are important, the quality of your presentation and of the person delivering it, your selection of a door-opener product, and the particular market you're pursuing all make an enormous difference in your results. Much of this is every bit as true in P&C as in L&H, although fewer people in P&C seem aware of it, probably because there is less overall teleprospecting in P&C, which means there is less overall data from which to draw conclusions.

PRIMARY GROUP TO BENEFIT FROM THIS BOOK

This book is not about large-scale operations. Instead, it has been written mainly to help individual insurance agents to improve their incomes through teleprospecting. Although *others who can benefit from it* will be discussed later, *primarily* these pages are addressed to those who do their own calling and/or at times hire probably one or two others *under their direct control* to do it for them.

HOW THIS BOOK CAN HELP YOU—OVERVIEW

It will help you to *organize* your teleprospecting, to define your overall *and specific* goals, and it will powerfully support you in achieving those goals, with special attention to:

1. Hiring Outside Teleprospectors

If you decide to use outside teleprospectors, it will help you to locate and hire those most likely to be truly appropriate to your needs, and to bring out the best in them.

2. Paperwork

Nor is it necessary to be eaten alive by paperwork, in connection with each call. How much information do you really *need*? Specifically, *what* do you need, and why? It's been said that research comes in two sizes: too much and too little. Too often, the same can be said of write-ups on teleprospecting calls.

3. Correspondence

Probably your related correspondence can be better than it is now. With only a few notes from the call integrated into a basic form follow-up letter, there's a lot you can do to begin firming up this initially very tenuous relationship. Because each appointment or even solid lead is so hard to obtain, when you also go to the expense of following up by mail, that follow-up should maximize its potential.

Preapproach letters also are often not what they could be, in terms of supporting your overall campaign. Why should I even accept the subsequent phone call which the letter promises will come? *Tell* me why—in the letter!

4. All Alone, or Yea Team!

Is it better to work as an individual or in teams? And if you do decide to work in a team, do you want your partner's expertise to supplement or to complement yours?

5. Service Firms—Yes or No?

If you are considering a service firm, this book will help you to understand the pros and cons. If you do go outside, it will help you to select which firm to employ and to monitor your results with far more sophistication than you probably have now. If it's not working out as you had hoped, it will help you to locate the source of the problem. Is it in you, or in the outside organization—and, wherever it is, what's the best way to handle it? More on this will appear in the next chapter.

OTHERS WHO CAN BENEFIT FROM THIS BOOK

But others, in addition to individual insurance salespeople, can also benefit from these pages.

Because large groups are composed of individuals, managers of large teleprospecting operations who implement what is recommended in these pages on improving individual performance will quantifiably improve their overall results.

Especially if your organization is a *multiservice* outside operation, it is probably apparent to you that insurance appointments are generally considerably more difficult to obtain than sales appointments for other products. This book will help you improve results for your insurance clients, while also facilitating more effective communication between your organization and the insurance professionals you serve. This more effective communication will not only ease friction once a project is underway, it can also give you a definite competitive edge in the initial sales presentations you make to the insurance professionals you hope will subscribe to your services.

If you are a freelance telephone solicitor—one of the many thousands who turn to cold calling when they need a few extra dollars—these pages can help you to succeed in one of the toughest and best paying telephone soliciting specialties in the country!

Although all of the material here focuses on *insurance* cold calling, some of it is universal and therefore applicable to a far broader range of products. If you are not in the insurance business and think you've already read everything anyone could possibly write about teleprospecting in your particular product or service area, if you pick up this book, you'll probably be pleasantly surprised by how much new material you will discover.

SUCCESSFUL TECHNIQUES CAN BE TAUGHT

Successful insurance teleprospecting techniques *can* be taught. You, or those working for you, can—*if you understand and work with the process*—pick up a source even as generic as a telephone directory, *even in target areas as tough and oversolicited as New York City* and, in a matter of hours, start filling in the blank spaces in your appointment book. If you stay with the process, some of these new contacts will definitely become clients. I know this because I've heard it all over the country, and have done it myself, repeatedly, while also training others whose subsequent success has been comparable to mine.

ADDITIONAL BENEFITS

If you conscientiously apply the guidelines in this book, unless you are already phenomenally adept in this area, you will substantially reduce your cost per sale because you will make far better use of the time either you or someone you've hired spends on the phone, very largely because you will be far better prepared before you begin.

You will also spend considerably less time on trial and error, hit or miss. Because you will recognize why something isn't working much sooner, you will know far more quickly when and where to cut your losses and move on to something more productive; you'll know when and how to revise a bad presentation, when to dump a bad list, a bad calling area, and/or a bad product ("bad" in terms of not catching the interest of those whose interest you seek to capture).

Of equal importance to all of the above—*you will feel considerably more comfortable with the entire teleprospecting process.* You will also feel, quite simply, happier. In addition to what tangibly enhanced success can do for your bank account, it is also an extraordinary morale booster!

_____

POWERFUL SUBJECT INTERCONNECTIONS—REMEMBER THE INDEX!

Because each component of the teleprospecting process is so deeply interconnected with all the others, to focus on any one necessarily brings up others; as an old subject comes up in a new context, often new information is added. Therefore, any time you seek more information on any one particular topic, for *complete* coverage, be sure to use the index.

CHAPTER **2**

Teleprospecting's Place in Overall Goal Planning

SPECIFIC GOALS

Specifically, what are your goals? *To sell insurance* is far too general an answer. You need much more clarity; for example, you plan to sell how much of what kind of insurance to whom, within what time frame, and *how do you intend to find your buyers*?

According to Paul Poulos, whose predominantly P&C three rural agencies—two in Vermont and one in New Hampshire—recently did slightly in excess of $6 million in combined premiums, "Having specific goals not only helps producers channel their resources more effectively, it also offers checkpoints. If what's been targeted is not being achieved, the deficiency shows up more quickly in a defined structure. This means that the problems can be resolved, the larger projects put back on track, that much sooner."

"TARGET GOALS" AND "PROCESS GOALS" DEFINED

Getting and keeping projects on track is very much of what goal planning is designed to facilitate.

Generally, I divide goals into two categories: *target* goals define *what* you want; *process* goals define, step by step, *how* you intend to get it. Each target goal is always supported by X number (it varies from project to project) of process goals; *always*, major objectives are reached step by step by step.

TARGET GOALS AND PROCESS GOALS—SWITCHING SEQUENCE

Among those who take teleprospecting's potential seriously, target goals are not always the first consideration. Sometimes the *process* goal of a successful cold-calling operation takes priority in the initial planning. Because teleprospecting has such power as a new client source, the question becomes: Which target goals are teleprospecting most likely to support? Thus the *process* determines the larger objectives, rather than the other way around. Although target goals which evolve through this criterion are not always what they would have been had the reality of finding buyers not been a critical consideration, it may help to remember that often a perfectly respectable survival response to not getting what you want is wanting what you can get!

THE SAD SAGA OF THE WOULD-BE FINANCIAL PLANNER

A woman I once worked for was determined to succeed as a financial planner, but it wasn't happening. Although possibly her skills in this area were exceptional, the bottom line was, she wasn't getting the clients. Her original referral base—never large to begin with—had run dry. The cold calling was not succeeding, neither were the mass mailings, and networking could have taken years, with no guarantees.

She was also an insurance agent. Had she invested the same energy in this area which she invested in trying to make it in financial planning, she could have gotten clients, some of whom probably would eventually have used her financial planning skills. But this wasn't how she wanted to do it.

Eventually, she left the business.

REALISTIC TELEPROSPECTING OBJECTIVES

The point is, where available transportation can take you is often a perfectly valid consideration in determining where you want to go.

There are places an effective teleprospecting operation can take you, and places it can't. Understanding which is which is critically important if you are to integrate this very powerful resource effectively into your overall game plan. More on what you may and may not reasonably expect of teleprospecting will be explored in subsequent chapters.

IMMEDIATE-, MEDIUM-, AND LONG-RANGE GOALS

Time frames are also important. If you try to reach in a week goals which require a month, you've set yourself up for extraordinary stress and failure. Certain kinds of teleprospecting appointments are relatively quick and easy to obtain; so are the sales you will make from them, while others—both the appointment and the sale—require considerably more time and effort. In the beginning, until seeds planted earlier begin to mature, if you haven't planned for short-range appointments/sales to fill the interval while you pursue medium- or long-range objectives, your appointment book—and bank account!—can start looking awfully empty.

EXAMPLE OF CLEAR GOAL ORIENTATION

Two of the clearest goal-oriented salespeople I ever worked for functioned as a team. They split their expenses and income 50-50. I was one of two teleprospectors, each of us working for the team one day a week.

Their *immediate* process goal in a target goal of X amount in new business each month was to fill one "field day" each week with *first-time* appointments garnered through teleprospecting, to maintain a steady flow of relatively fast albeit small sales. A primary *medium-range* process goal was to fill a second day each week with first-time teleprospected appointments in search of slower but considerably larger sales. *Long range*, they planned to remain in the insurance business, focusing on L&H individual and group sales, primarily in Manhattan, where they shared an office, but also extending into a certain section of New Jersey, where the male partner lived with his family.

Although the teleprospecting component was critically important, it was—as always—part of a larger game plan. However, because both brokers were true believers in the power of cold calling, the decision to use teleprospecting came *before* the target goals of *what* they wanted to sell were established. The larger game plan—*the products they initially offered and the particular potential-client groups they pursued*—were meticulously selected to capitalize on which doors teleprospecting could probably open.

POOR PROCESS GOAL PLANNING

Sometimes *process* goal planning is so haphazard, there's no way even the best teleprospecting skills could rescue the operation. I bring this up because over the years I have seen so many salespeople whose target goals were well conceived but their process planning was, at best, uneven. As a result, the success for which they worked so hard was considerably less than it could/should have been—repeatedly.

HORRIBLE EXAMPLES!

One producer who generally did very well in face-to-face selling *lost* the only copies of four or five appointments I had gotten for him, not through some cruel twist of fate, but through the most unbelievably chaotic desk mess I've ever seen. Two weeks later, he lost two out of another batch, but the second time, I had outsmarted him. I had photocopied them, keeping the copies with *me*!

And then there was the salesman who left for the field before I came in, leaving me his open appointment book, his high hopes, and a chamber of commerce membership list to call from, about 80 percent of which consisted of other insurance agencies!

I also remember the agent who left me a message instructing me to call from his dollar-a-name Dun & Bradstreet superelite supertargeted cards so that he would have some appointments as soon as he got back from his vacation during which he could not be reached—but I wound up resorting to the phone book, because only the salesman and God knew where the cards were stashed!

None of these people was stupid or new to the business; they were merely very poorly organized—and they paid for it!

Another example of poor planning—but through inexperience, not carelessness—was the enthusiastic young salesman who had just bought his first list of names: ZIP Code–based, covering one of the most expensive residential areas in Manhattan.

"It won't work!" I squawked.

By the end of the evening, he decided the problem was me; I had been unable to come up with even one wealthy person willing to see him for a free life insurance review.

I've heard it so often, I'm willing to believe it: if you make enough calls, you'll sell some insurance. But with a process as ill conceived as the one just described, would even a lifetime of renewals begin to pay off the original teleprospecting investment? How much wiser to aim for a group statistically more amenable to insurance cold calling or, if he insisted on pursuing that particular market, to at least find a specific product which might catch its imagination!

PENSION SALESMEN SEEKING ACCOUNTANTS

The very clearly defined long-range goal of two older, considerably more experienced salesmen was to design and manage pensions for small businesses in the New York area. Pensions, period. Nothing else. But too often they had submitted proposals they thought were excellent, only to be shot down in the eleventh hour by their potential clients' accountants, often capriciously and arbitrarily, both salesmen believed.

Their immediate *teleprospecting* goal could not have been clearer. It was to set lunch dates with accountants, then—this time in cooperation with the accountants—go back to square one.

Up front, they warned me to expect only a fraction of the success I was used to. However, they said, they believed that even one or two solid contacts as ongoing referral sources would eventually more than justify the initial teleprospecting expense. For whatever reasons, I found accountants among the two or three toughest groups I'd ever tried to reach. *Doctors and lawyers were easier.*

I got better as I went along. More were willing to listen to me, and some who said to call back in a few weeks or to send information seemed genuinely open to further discussion. Some of the improvement came from merely getting into the swing of the process, but a lot came from trial and error.

I made subtle revisions in the script; I made notes on objections I hadn't expected; and then I tracked down my salespeople for answers on handling them. Once when I turned a call over to one of my salesman, I stood in the doorway of his office and listened to his end of the conversation. Hearing him gave me more information than I needed, but more was better than not enough, which was what I'd had when I started.

I learned that the best time to reach the accountants was around four—or later—in the afternoon, an experience not at all limited to the New York area. This was not necessarily best in terms of how *many* I reached, but it was a *good* time. Often they were back in their offices beginning to unwind after a long day, picking up their own phones and in relatively mellow states of mind.

I was also surprised to find that very few were upset if I managed to wangle a number from their secretaries and call them at a client's office. Perhaps this was because the client had no idea who I was, so the call itself merely suggested that the accountant was in demand.

RESULTS

By the end of the first full week (20 hours) of calling, I had made three appointments (only one for lunch). Two other accountants, unwilling to make appointments through me, talked to my salespeople by phone but only because my salespeople happened to be in the office when these particular calls were made. One agreed to an appointment; this brought the total number for the 20 hours of calling, to four.

Had neither of my salesmen been in, probably both of the calls I referred to the one who was available would have washed out. Most reactions to cold calls are very much mood of the moment; in that moment, the contact is either embraced or lost.

A number of others among the literally hundreds of accountants I called probably also would have talked with my salespeople, had my salespeople been accessible in that moment. But most of the time while I called, they were in the field. With no one immediately available, the built-in tenuousness of most cold-calling connections washed away the opportunity.

In these circumstances, in a market this tough, with this much potential riding on each contact relative to their ultimate target goal, more focused process goal planning could definitely have made a substantial difference in the final figures.

ALTERNATIVE APPROACHES

Their overall teleprospecting goal was to set up appointments with accountants. A number of alternatives to support this were available:

1. With prospects this difficult to reach and each one holding this much potential, the salesmen could have done the calling themselves. Often the accountants had specific questions, which I could not answer. The right answers could have *shown*—rather than merely told—the accountants that the pension designers were, indeed, specialists of a caliber worth meeting.

2. They could have called *for awhile* for appointments, but also for information to help train an outsider to be immediately more effective; for example, they would have known right away that late afternoons were best for quality time.

3. Either of the salesmen could have worked directly with an outside teleprospector, possibly even in the same room. While the salesman did paperwork, the outsider could have called, sifting through screeners but immediately turning over to the salesman any accountant willing to talk, allowing the salesman to close the appointment.

4. They could have hired an outsider who would do his or her own closing, but kept at least one salesman in the general vicinity for instant backup on any call where an accountant unwilling to make an appointment through the teleprospector *was* willing to at least talk to one of the salesmen, *in the mood of the moment.*

UNREALIZED POTENTIAL RESULTS

The final numbers illustrate the salesmen's underutilization of the teleprospecting process in support of their larger target goals. Their *teleprospecting* goals should have included, clearly stated, not just appointments but, *under these circumstances, with an investment of this magnitude*, as many appointments as possible, each as qualified as possible. Certainly they *hoped* for this, but hope is not enough.

If we exclude the appointment closed by the salesman only because by chance he was available at the right time, we have a total of three. If the follow-up with those who seemed open to later contact were responsibly handled, probably the total would eventually exceed three, but "probably" doesn't count. The only concrete number we have to work with is three.

With only three appointments in 20 hours' calling, if even one more had been made because the outsider was better prepared going in, or the salesman had been making his own calls or had at least been available to close for the outsider—that single extra appointment would represent an increased return on investment of approximately 33 percent. *Three* additional appointments would have *doubled* the return, cut in *half* the cost per appointment! Nor is there anything here to suggest that only three more would have been the maximum possible.

UNNECESSARY STRESS

A second indication of inadequate process planning was obvious in the stress surrounding the whole project. It was not constructive; it was exhausting. As is very common, because they had waited too long to begin, they were under tremendous pressure to produce immediately.

CONCLUSION

With apologies for telling a story without an ending, I don't know what happened to them. When I went back to the same agency several months later to work for someone else, the pension designers were no longer there.

However, whether trying to connect with accountants through teleprospecting was a good idea to begin with is questionable. In Islip, New York, salesman Al Levine works with quite a few accountants—and tax attorneys.

"I chartered a boat," he offers cheerfully. "I invited accountants and tax attorneys, *and their wives*, for drinks, dancing, and a tax seminar. Some of the accountants were employed by the Big-6 firms. First I called; then I sent formal invitations.

"More than 80 people attended. Including the liquor, the evening cost me about $5,000. Shortly afterward, as a direct result of that evening, I wrote two large cases. I still do business with many others who attended.

"Most salespeople who do seminars rent a hotel room, with wine and cheese," he adds, "but that's not enough. You have to be creative!"

However, although sometimes "creative" is enough, this is not always the issue. Kickbacks are illegal, yet others interviewed said that not uncommonly, in lieu of actual cash, expensive "gifts" are exchanged for productive referrals.

This is not to suggest that teleprospecting *cannot* work with accountants, but as explored in far greater depth in the next chapter, *not everyone you'd like to do business with is equally accessible through teleprospecting*. Who to pursue is often a major consideration.

PLAN IT OUT, WRITE IT DOWN!

However, whatever your goals, and whatever process you have in mind for achieving them, if you are a reasonably well-trained professional salesperson, it's probably safe to assume you've already been advised to write down all of it, not just to think it through, but to *write it down*. Write down

1. Your target goals: immediate, short range, and long range
2. Your process goals: step by step by very carefully thoroughly thought-out step, write down how you intend to achieve each target goal

None of this means you can't modify your plans if subsequent experiences change your perspective, but if you use this process, you will at least have something *to* modify, within the continuing clarity of *a* support structure.

RESISTANCE

If you're like the vast majority of insurance agents I've known over the years, by now you're probably feeling resistant. Most salespeople, by nature, want to sell. They spark to the presentation, the close. Very few enjoy the often tedious process of finding potential buyers. And most feel they already have far too much paperwork. The idea of adding to it by actually writing out their goals is, conservatively stated, a turnoff.

But write them down, anyway.

WHY WRITING DOWN GOALS IS IMPORTANT

Write them down because studies on subsequent success overwhelmingly support the belief that—all else being reasonably equal—as a statistical group, those who put their goals in writing eventually become far more successful than those who don't.

There are several theories on why this is so important. Some say it not only focuses your thinking, but also helps to make your goals second nature, to make them an integral part of who you are so that automatically, even your smallest thought or action incorporates and thereby moves you closer to them.

Another theory is that the process of putting goals into writing invokes a metaphysical component, something akin to the beliefs of those who support what today is often called creative visualization. The basic precepts of creative visualization are not at all new; they are reflected in some of the earliest artwork of our most ancient ancestors who, when their goal was to kill a buffalo, "wrote it down" in pictures on the walls of their caves. Thousands of years later, this process was dubbed *sympathetic magic*; picture the deed done, and it will be done.

But *how* it works is not the issue. What matters is, when you write down your goals, you tap into some of the oldest—and also most modern—success-oriented belief systems in existence!

So, why not? Picture the appointment made, the sale closed. Picture the complete process, all the way from square one through whatever it is you'd most like to achieve. And as part of the process, picture yourself with a superb teleprospecting operation!

PRIMARY TELEPROSPECTING GOAL

Your primary teleprospecting goal, concisely stated, is to maximize every dollar/hour you invest, in support of your overall selling objectives.

COST/BENEFIT CONSIDERATIONS

Only you can decide what constitutes an acceptable cost/benefit teleprospecting ratio; it all depends on how it all fits into your overall game plan. Because they had only one product, the pension salesmen believed that connecting with accountants justified the extraordinary expense. Others in the same agency also designed pensions—but offered this service in conjunction with a number of others. On different occasions, two had me pursue pension design appointments directly with small businesses, not through accountants, at a considerably lower cost per appointment. I know that at least one of these did turn into a moderate sale, and there were others, although smaller.

GETTING IT TOGETHER

If you've decided to use teleprospecting to open new doors for you, the following will help you to focus your thinking as you integrate it into your larger objectives.

Many years ago in my checkered career, I was a newspaper writer. When I sat down to analyze for this book what I had been doing intuitively that worked so well in the teleprospecting, I realized that much of it was rooted in the newspaper training.

WHO, WHAT, WHERE, WHEN, AND WHY?

Even if your only exposure to newspaper writing has been to read it after it was in print, you've probably still heard of the five W's: Who, What, Where, When, and Why. Every news story was supposed to include answers to these questions, although not necessarily in this order.

Invariably, in first-time meetings with new clients, the five W's were very much in my thoughts, clearly reflected in the questions I asked. In the beginning, I was surprised to see how few otherwise sharp salespeople had really thought through all five:

1. WHO do you want to call?

2. WHAT specific products do you want to sell, and WHAT are you willing to sell as door-openers for larger sales?

3. WHERE do you want to reach those you call, at home, or at work? And WHERE do you want to sell? How broad are your geographical boundaries?

4. WHEN do you want to call—certain times of day, days of the week, and, in some cases, particular seasons are better than others; for example, travel agents will have less time for you during peak vacation travel months, and to start calling accountants in late March or early April doesn't make much sense.

5. WHY should the particular prospect you are calling buy your product and buy it from you rather than from any one of a hundred other salespeople?

The primary focus of this chapter was on major teleprospecting target and process goal questions. In the next, we'll work on some answers.

CHAPTER 3

Matching Market Segments With Compatible "Door-opener" Strategies

APPROPRIATE PROSPECTS

To achieve results which will justify your teleprospecting investment, you need *prospects* who

1. are likely to be interested in what you're offering
2. can afford it
3. are accessible by phone
4. are or eventually probably will be in a position to buy more and/or to refer you to others also likely to become both clients and sources of additional referrals

Albeit this last element is an advantage in P&C, it is more important in life, where the commission structure makes an ongoing new client flow crucial if the producer is to survive more than a year or so.

WHO BUYS WHAT KIND OF INSURANCE—AND HOW?

Because a very wide variety of people buy a very broad range of insurance products, in formulating the process goals to support your particular target goals, two key questions emerge:

1. WHO buys the kind of insurance you sell?
2. HOW do they buy it?

An overview of WHO buys WHAT, and HOW, follows, all in the context of potential teleprospecting effectiveness.

THE PYRAMID—VIEW FROM THE BOTTOM

If you picture a pyramid *consisting of people who buy insurance*, at the bottom you'll find those whose purchases are minimal, usually barebones personal L&H and P&C (most commonly car insurance). They respond to TV, mail, or print ads; or they sometimes walk into storefront offices or banks which sell insurance; or perhaps they participate in the cost if they have group plans where they work. And in case it's foreign to your experience, there are still places where certain insurance salespeople "hang around," selling whatever they can to whoever might come along and buy it.

"He's not that guy who's always hanging around here, is he?" a prospect once asked me. No, I assured her, the CLU with the Manhattan skyline poshly carpeted office for whom I was calling did not "hang around" anywhere; he worked by appointment only.

This bottom-level group is not fertile ground for teleprospectors. Even with a halfway decent sale, you'd still need many more to balance out your total soliciting investment. Also, both by-phone and by-appointment selling usually require eventual add-on and/or referral business to offset the initial cost. In this group, additional business potential is too minimal to justify anything.

PYRAMID CONTINUED—MORE FERTILE GROUND

At this next-higher socioeconomic level, although money is still tight, far more potential buyers seek more varied and/or extensive coverage. More purchase "packages," each containing a number of policies, collectively intended to meet a variety of specific needs for each individual purchaser. These prospects also buy through a variety of sources, but now those sources include far more individual agents who have made efforts—usually by phone, mail, referrals, or, more directly, through getting out and meeting a *lot* of people—to contact them.

"COLD-CALL COWBOYS"

However, according to Walter V. Worsham III, CLU, ChFC, a 20-year L&H veteran producer in Augusta, Georgia, "to make even a modest living working this market, you must see a *lot* of people. You just keep dialing; don't let your fingers rest. Most of those who do it—we call them 'cold-call cowboys'—get burned out pretty quick."

Walt does cold call, but he successfully targets a considerably more affluent clientele. The specific teleprospecting strategies he employs will be discussed later in this chapter.

SMALLER GROUP WITH MORE TO PROTECT SPENDS ACCORDINGLY

Continuing upward, an even smaller group has more to protect and spends accordingly. Some is personal, some commercial. Climb another few steps. In addition to extensive personal and general commercial needs, these buyers also have far more specialized commercial needs, and the money to meet those needs.

THE APEX

At the top—the apex of the pyramid—are the true believers, with money and a cornucopia of personal and commercial insurance requirements, some paying astronomical annual premiums.

With one exception, I recommend that you forget the apex. That kind of wealth is too well insulated. Even if you did slip through and reach half-a-dozen multimillionaires, it's highly unlikely that any of them would actually see you!

The one exception is teleprospecting your way into giant corporations, an option which will be explored later in this chapter.

NOT QUITE THE APEX—TELEPROSPECTING VERSUS NETWORKING

Staying with mainly personal insurance prospects strictly in terms of potential teleprospecting success, let's look more closely at prospects reasonably near the top, those who, although not superrich, are nonetheless way up there on income.

Anyone can hit the lottery, but buying tickets is not really an "investment." It's gambling, against enormous odds. At this socioeconomic level, potential clients seeking insurance virtually always work with salespeople they already know or who have been recommended, usually through friends, relatives, neighbors, or business associates—very commonly accountants and lawyers—all of whom turn the circle back into itself by opening doors only for insurance professionals they already know.

If the adventurous side of your nature is such that you still want to try, remember it's not "just numbers." Pay careful attention to your *product* as well as your telephone presentation. Most of those I called at home for the young salesman with the expensive residential section list picked up their own phones, so they were not unreachable. Instead, they were merely uninterested, but the product—simply life insurance—was far too bland, especially with a pitch as flat as yesterday's Pepsi.

I wouldn't do it again without a considerably more targeted presentation, probably one built around a specific offbeat product designed to cut taxes, which their regular insurance broker, accountant, and/or lawyer may have overlooked.

WHO YOU KNOW

Of course, who you know is important in any profession, but especially among insurance salespeople. The people you socialize with on weekends quite commonly determine those with whom you'll do business the following week.

"Monday mornings are not a good time to cold call," offers Antoinette Hondroulis, based on her teleprospecting experiences in New Orleans, Louisiana. "On Monday mornings, the gentlemen you'd like to reach tend to be occupied *processing whatever business was conducted while they were sailing or playing golf over the weekend.*"

And these are the potential clients who *are* reachable through teleprospecting; even among these, insurance professionals who network have a definite advantage.

But among "rich" potential clients, networking is more than an advantage; it's virtually a requirement.

THE APEX EXCEPTION—PURSUING GIANT CORPORATIONS

Giant corporations can definitely become apex clients through teleprospecting, although most spread their insurance purchases to include a number of different carriers, seeking the best possible arrangement with each, sometimes switching as one comes up with a better product than another.

Because these corporations are ultimately answerable to stockholders, if your pitch is *extremely* well presented, largely in terms of WHAT you want to sell and WHY it is special, on the offchance that you really do have a better mousetrap, some of those with the power to buy business insurance from you will consider it part of their jobs to at least meet with you.

COMPETITION SOMETIMES "UNFAIR"

However, even if you do get through the door, the competition remains extraordinary, and not always "fair."

There are horror stories: agents who came in through cold calls and spent weeks—even months—preparing proposals so exceptional the client did indeed buy them—but not from the agents who had prepared them. Ultimately, the clients went back to the inner circle of vendors with whom they were already working. Perhaps this also happens at lower levels of the pyramid, where the stakes are lower, but if so, I'm unaware of it.

HIGH COST PER CORPORATE APPOINTMENT

In addition, in cold calling giants, as opposed to even a "lukewarm" referral, the cost per appointment is usually high; you'll need either to do it yourself or to hire someone sharp. Remember, people generally feel more comfortable doing business with others whom they feel are like themselves. If you're dealing at the vice presidential level of a giant corporation, do not use as a calling card someone who sounds as if you're paying him or her only a dollar or so over minimum wage. To do so wastes everyone's time.

BUILT-IN DIFFICULTY IN REACHING THE APPROPRIATE PERSON

And even if you are on track with both your product and the cold caller presenting it, you're still dealing with what seems to be an intrinsic, time-consuming difficulty in connecting with the right person. Expensive lists which are supposed to include the right name are often wrong, partly because of personnel changes but also partly because, although the people do not change, quite commonly their specific responsibilities do.

EXTRA-TOUGH SCREENERS

Furthermore, you'll run into some of the tightest screeners you'll ever encounter. Even those willing to put you through often can't because the person you seek really is very rarely simply sitting at his or her desk alone, free to accept phone calls, which means you must call again—and again. Leaving messages can backfire—but more on this is covered in Chapter 7.

COMMON OBJECTION

When you do get through, *I don't have time, now, call back in a month* is a common objection. And it's true. A *good* teleprospector will sometimes set the appointment anyway, subject to much later confirmation, but the confirmation call often requires a complete reselling job, which may or may not be successful.

LARGE CORPORATION P&C X-DATES

If you're thinking of setting up an operation to gather *large-corporation* P&C X-dates, you won't need callers quite as sophisticated as those you would need actually to close appointments for you when the time is right, but "monkeys-with-scripts" are a debatable choice. *At this level*, you are often competing with some of the best teleprospectors in the business.

However, if this is your goal—go for it! *But know what you're up against.*

MOST PURCHASERS ARE NOT GIANTS

However, it may help to realize that only 15 percent of the population works for these giant concerns; *most* producers who sell group coverage work with considerably smaller clients.

PYRAMID REVISITED—THE MIDDLE IS BEST!

Meanwhile, back at the pyramid—in terms of potential teleprospecting direct return on investment—the middle is not only the largest segment, it is the best! This does not mean middle-income or midsized companies only, although both are included. It means, for business insurance, the *whole* pyramid midsection, ranging from slightly below the large corporations all the way to mom and pop candy stores. In personal coverage, it includes the whole income range from six figures per annum all the way down to anyone in a position to buy from you and eventually give you worthwhile add-on business and/or referrals with the same potential.

ADDITIONAL MARKET SEGMENT BREAKDOWNS

The middle of the pyramid covers a lot of territory. And the process of picking a particular target group is not always tidy.

"If everybody you dealt with were, for example, a 25-year-old female schoolteacher," offers Walt Worsham, in Georgia, "it would all be a lot easier, but life doesn't work like that. There are big differences—age, money, profession, time. You have to be flexible in what you're offering, able to 'pivot.'"

Certainly, the broader the range of people you can serve, the better, and the more of each individual's needs you can meet, the less time and money necessary to pursue new clients.

WHERE AND HOW TO BEGIN

However, everybody still begins a teleprospecting campaign on a particular square marked "GO," a first choice on which markets to pursue, and which approaches they feel are likely to catch the interest of those particular markets.

WITH WHOM DO YOU FEEL MOST COMFORTABLE?

Selecting a market with which you feel especially comfortable has a way of reflecting itself back in prospects likely to feel more comfortable with you and, consequently, more likely to buy from you.

In Fort Collins, Colorado, salesman Randy Crawford works predominantly with older people. He likes them, gets along well with them. His primary expertise is in products which meet their retirement years' special needs.

A woman I worked for in New York City with a B.A. in comparative literature did especially well with small bookstores. Her lead product was deeply discounted personal L&H, offered in cooperation with a professional association to which most of the booksellers belonged. But once through the door, she sometimes found nice business group opportunities.

SOMETIMES YOUR MARKET SELECTS YOU—THE WHERE-YOU-LIVE FACTOR

But sometimes the area itself defines its own specialized needs. Although, according to Metropolitan Life agent Joe Olesky in Belle Vernon, Pennsylvania, "We have a four-lane highway that goes anywhere," like Randy Crawford in Colorado, Joe also focuses on the elderly, but Joe's options were considerably more limited than Randy's. In Belle Vernon, older people are, by far, the dominant market.

"It's a depressed area," Joe explains, "a mill and coal-mining town, devastated in the 1980s. The young people left to search for jobs. Only the elderly are left. We work with an estate attorney, wills and trusts. We do a lot of estate planning; tax planning."

Joe grew up nearby; he feels at home there.

BLUE COLLAR/WHITE COLLAR—UNION/NON-UNION

A New York City teleprospector with a blue-collar background did quite well setting up *personal* pension design appointments with owners of blue-collar businesses, which brings up another issue. Although *some* white-collar businesses are unionized, most aren't, while most blue-collar businesses are. Unions mean union benefits, which undermine your potential for certain *kinds* of sales in this group, but not all shops are unionized, and as the teleprospector just mentioned proved with his results, often owners of either union or non-union shops are perfectly valid personal lines prospects.

WHO'S ACCESSIBLE BY PHONE?

Wherever you start, to teleprospect, you need people who are accessible by phone. This is an area you'll need to think through, and possibly experiment with, relative to where you live. I was delighted by how many chiropractors picked up their own phones, while more often than not, calling locksmiths connected me with answering devices.

DOOR-OPENER CATEGORIES

Once you've decided which market segment you'd like to focus on initially, playing the odds on how your teleprospecting efforts are likely to be most productive requires some major decisions on how to approach that segment.

Basically, there are six primary teleprospecting door-opener approaches. Some will work much better in one geographical area rather than another. For example, the reputation of your agency generally works better in small towns; in big cities, without a referral, other alternatives are usually more effective.

The following list presents the most commonly used door-openers in no particular order of effectiveness or common usage, except for number 6, at the bottom because it belongs there:

1. Special expertise on a catchy specific product

2. A representation of other special expertise especially relevant to a particular prospect's needs

3. Convincing the prospect that *possibly* you can do better than your competition on price or coverage for the same price or service (service is a major issue in P&C door-openers)

4. The reputation of the agency you work through

5. A certain pizazz over the phone; in essence, your "lead product" is yourself

6. "I'm conducting a survey"

CATCHY LEAD PRODUCTS

If you decide to try the catchy lead product approach (either a new product or catchy new approach to an old product), what you offer can be either personal or business. There's no reason why you can't reach into both categories, nor are you limited to either L&H or P&C.

You may want to hedge your bets by choosing two or more products, at least until you're sure you've found one that works. But no matter how many you choose, virtually always it's best to present each one separately, each with its own campaign geared to its own market.

If you are doing your own calling or have hired someone especially sharp to do it for you, sometimes you *can* switch pitches in midstream if a prospect is not warming to your initial offering, but this is an exception rather than a rule.

INSURANCE COMPANY BROKERS AS SOURCES FOR CATCHY LEAD PRODUCTS

If you feel a little short on catchy new products, insurance trade magazines, such as *American Agent & Broker* (P&C) or *Life Insurance Selling* and/or *L&H Insurance Sales* (for L&H products), sometimes list them as a regular feature. In addition, when major insurance companies come out with them, often brokers *representing the insurance companies* cold call individual agencies to let them know something new is available.

In Charlotte, North Carolina, Laurie Prevette, RHU, with Equity Brokerage, Inc., was recently heavily involved in the promotion of a new *standard* life insurance program for people with adverse medical histories. This, in the right market, could be a very effective door opener, indeed.

In Louisville, Kentucky, Irving H. Shaw, CLU, ChHC, RHU, LUTCF, chief executive officer of Shaw American Companies, is typical of many others throughout the country in keeping very much abreast of what's new and also of any changes which might give one already existing product a price advantage over a comparable offering by a competitor. Irv also collects data on what individual producers feel *should* be out there—and passes it on to major companies. "If there's something I feel would sell well to consumers and none of the major companies has it, I'll ask them to create it."

"SUPERMARKET" BROKERS VERSUS "BOUTIQUE"

In Fort Worth, Texas, independent agent Suzanna Edwards distinguishes those who offer a wide range of products from those who specialize in a narrower range. For relatively new producers, she recommends starting with those who offer the "supermarket" broader selection. "But after awhile," she explains, "you learn which 'boutique' to approach for which particular specialized need."

DIAL-A-DOOR OPENER!

Irv Shaw, of Shaw American Companies, in Kentucky, has offered to give any interested agent contact information on other brokers like Irv in other parts of the country, not only to facilitate staying abreast of what's new the moment it becomes available, but also to share input on what producers would like to see *become* available. As a resource for not only locating but possibly even designing your own "catchy new products," this is an option you may want to exercise.

When warned that he might find himself fielding a *lot* of calls, Irv nonetheless tendered his toll-free number:

1 (800) 626-5888

Louisville, Kentucky, operates on Eastern Standard (or Daylight Savings) Time.

SPECIAL EXPERTISE IN PARTICULAR BUSINESSES OR PROFESSIONS

Other special expertise (other than expertise on specific lead products) often shows up as, "We do a lot of work with _____." Fill in the blank: What *kinds* of businesses are you calling, for example, video stores, or are you categorizing by profession, such as, dentists?

MORE SPECIAL EXPERTISE BY PROFESSION—ASSOCIATIONS

If your inclination is to categorize/call according to profession, you may want to explore association insurance. In this context, "associations" are organizations which have made arrangements with major insurance carriers to discount coverage for the organizations' members; in essence, association insurance allows individuals to purchase individual insurance at group rates. Here, your special expertise is in what is available at the special prices.

In case you're not familiar with association insurance, the catch 22 is that much of it is easily cancelable. The upside is, from your first meeting, you will review existing coverage to discover where the association coverage fits in with whatever the prospect already has, with the goal of eventually replacing everything cancelable, while upgrading the rest.

"ACCORDING TO OUR RECORDS"

Certain group pension information is in the public domain. When you approach a potential client with information on his or her company's pension, showing how what you are offering is superior, this demonstration of "special expertise" *on the prospect's specific situation* is usually a powerful attention-getter.

MORE SPECIAL EXPERTISE—FREE FINANCIAL ADVICE

"Hi. I'm with the Joe Jones Company (use your *agency*, not the name of an insurance company). We specialize in cutting taxes." Since these are generally more sizzle than steak, their effectiveness rests about 99 percent in the pitch and how it's presented. Both will be dealt with in more detail in Chapter 12, which focuses on designing and delivering telephone presentations.

WILL THE *REAL* EXPERT PLEASE STAND UP!

Special expertise is sometimes used as a door-opener when a *predominantly* L&H agency uses one, often on-premises, P&C agent to provide P&C service to the L&H agency's clients or when a *predominantly* P&C outfit has, perhaps, one L&H salesperson off in a bleak, windowless room somewhere. A competitive L&H or P&C agent *with an agency specializing in his or her area of expertise* can often do well with the claim of knowing much more than the poor lonely orphan the clients bought from when they bought P&C through a mainly L&H agency or L&H through a predominantly P&C agency.

PRICE AND/OR SERVICE ADVANTAGE

This is the primary door-opener—*across the board, throughout the country*—in most commercial P&C teleprospecting, but also effective in both personal and commercial L&H.

A surprisingly effective opening for those who pursue this route is, quite simply, "Are you *happy* (satisfied) with your current coverage/price/insurance representative?" Probably you will be delighted by how many are not and will actually be pleased with the opportunity to tell you why.

AGENCY REPUTATION

In small towns—even reasonably small cities—sometimes the reputation of a particular agency makes the agency itself a primary "lead product." In Richland, Washington, Karen Fruchtl, a part-time teleprospector who spends the rest of her time in customer service for the same agency she calls for, has been teleprospecting for the past two years. Richland is a town of approximately 40,000, about four hours from Tacoma. She calls into Richland for the Richland agency where she is based and also into two nearby towns, one in Oregon, for two other agencies owned by the same group that owns the Richland agency. All three towns have comparable populations.

SIMPLE, DIRECT APPROACH, WELL PRESENTED

Her presentation is unusually direct, consisting basically of "Hi. I'm Karen, from Spencer-Kinney Insurance. We do property and casualty. We do bonding. We have a life insurance department, a benefits department—."

Her results, she says, are uneven, but on balance, satisfactory. "Some days, in a four-hour calling block, there could be seven or eight appointments, or more, and on other days, none."

In essence, *her lead product is the agency itself*, but the agency is unusual. Established in 1948, some of its managerial and sales personnel today are third generation. *Most* of its business is P&C. Because the quality of the ongoing service is such a major component in satisfying P&C clients, this kind of stability is a valuable selling point.

In addition, Karen's telephone style is exceptional. With the solid background she acquired in customer service before she began teleprospecting, she comes across immediately as friendly, bright, and well informed, with a natural high, positive energy which in itself, predisposes listeners to take her seriously.

But whether her results would be better if her presentation were more targeted is an interesting question, one that might be worth some experimentation. However, at present, *her lead product is the agency itself*—and it works!

"I'M CONDUCTING A SURVEY"

Of course, there is the "survey." It's classic, starting out as though all you really want is information on the prospect's present coverage—but most people don't believe it. We're too sophisticated today, especially at the socioeconomic levels you're likely to be calling.

Or, if they *do* believe it, often they will feel betrayed—used—when you call back later to pursue your real goal.

In my experience, and among a *vast* majority of those I talked to, it's better to cut to the chase a lot sooner; to tell people virtually immediately why you're calling, and what you feel you can do for them.

CURRENT EVENTS ALWAYS VALID EXCUSE TO CALL

The last time Blue Cross and Blue Shield raised their rates in New York, a lot of small-business owners were deeply angry. It was a creamy time to call about better rates on group health insurance.

And following the October 1987 crash, for awhile lots of people suddenly took life insurance far more seriously than before.

Sensitizing yourself to recognizing current event/insurance tie-ins can give you a nice "hook." As you read/watch the news, ask yourself how what you're learning might affect insurance sales; how could you tie it into a succinct sales approach?

Of course, a current event in itself is not a door-opener. You still need one of the options just listed, but the current event can serve as a valuable enhancer.

HIGHER-RATED INSURANCE COMPANIES

Shari Halloran, an extraordinarily successful independent teleprospector in Topeka, Kansas, does very well emphasizing the safety of New York Life. Offering products by other S&P highly-rated companies is especially good today and probably will be for many years to come. You can open by asking prospects whether they are sure their present carrier is really safe.

WHAT WORKS WHERE—REGIONAL DIFFERENCES IN PERSONAL STYLE

In Rockford, Illinois, which is larger than the area Karen Fruchtl solicits but also a relatively small town, Ned Burns, an eight-year L&H veteran salesman, starts with a preapproach letter generally based on an event in the prospect's life, such as a promotion at work. He then calls with a directness apparently effective in Rockford, but whether this would get him enough appointments in larger, more competitive areas of the country is questionable.

"Let's talk about how these changes affect you in your everyday life," he suggests. "I have some ideas I'd like to share with you." Basically, the content of his presentation is that he's not selling anything; he'd just like to establish an initial personal contact, thereby laying the groundwork for possible *future* business.

Deliberately, Ned *avoids* any mention of a specific product. Although he has already volunteered in the letter that he sells life and health insurance, *the whole thrust of his telephone presentation is only to set up the appointment.*

In effect, his "lead product" is himself!

Like Karen Fruchtl in Washington, Ned has an especially good telephone style, conveying unusually good, positive energy.

"COLD" CALLS IN GEORGIA WARMED BY PRE-APPROACH NEWSLETTER

Walt Worsham, in Georgia, also presents as his lead product himself, but the tenor of his calls is different from Ned's.

Although, like many others, Walt uses pre-approach letters, which will be discussed in greater detail in Chapter 10, he also has a newsletter which he finds particularly effective.

"I send it once a month for maybe four or five months to businesspeople I'd especially like to have as clients. Usually, I send out about 300. It has my name and picture. The picture's very important. After awhile, they get used to receiving it, used to 'seeing' me. By the time I call, I'm not really a stranger anymore.

"Some show right away they're not interested, but that's okay. Usually I do get a positive response. We chat awhile. I talk to them about business continuation, deferred compensation, estate liquidity—total needs planning. What I'm really doing is *qualifying* them. When I go out on an appointment, I want to meet a *prospect*, not a *suspect*."

IN SUMMARY

In summary, if you live in an area where the reputation of your agency can open doors, or if, like both Ned and Walt, you're awfully good in how you present yourself, and this *style* works, then these door-openers are valid options for you, although you still might want to experiment in refining whatever you already have into even more effective approaches.

However, if your agency alone, no matter how well presented in a cold call, is not enough, and the style used by Ned and Walt is a washout, then the other options listed at the beginning of this section, which will all be explored in much greater depth in Chapter 12, will probably be the ones on which you'll concentrate.

CHAPTER 4

Tele*prospecting*/Tele*marketing* —Large-scale Regimented Versus Small-scale Personalized Cold Calling

WHY UNDERSTANDING TELEPROSPECTING OPTIONS IS IMPORTANT

When asked why an insurance professional should hire an outside service firm, the president of a very successful outside firm promptly responded, "Because cold calling is our business. It's not theirs; theirs is to sell insurance."

And yet, because the definitive responsibility for your success is ultimately yours, cold calling *is* your business. Whether you do it yourself, set up a full-scale in-house operation, hire a service firm, or hire an independent, you still need to understand what's happening. Otherwise, you cannot make informed choices, and *un*-informed choices—particularly when you're laying out your money as well as your time—can be expensive!

TELEPROSPECTING/TELEMARKETING OPERATIONS—RELATIVE SIZE

Distinctions between tele*marketing* and most tele*prospecting* calls extend beyond their separate *immediate* objectives of *product sales* through tele*marketing* and *appointments* through tele*prospecting*. Most tele*prospecting* operations are relatively small; relative, that is, to most tele*marketing* operations.

COST-EFFECTIVE TELEMARKETING OPERATIONS

To be cost effective, insurance tele*marketing* operations are generally large and highly sophisticated, with backup support in promotional material and in data collection and analysis to fine-tune their profitability, far beyond what individual agents could reasonably afford.

LICENSING REQUIREMENTS FOR INSURANCE-RELATED COLD CALLERS

Also, if you are selling an insurance *product* over the phone rather than merely making an *appointment* to sell a product, you must be a licensed insurance salesperson. You also must be licensed if you live in a state which limits *any* form of insurance soliciting to licensed salespeople only, which is the case in Kansas. And although as far as I was able to determine, no unlicensed solicitor has ever been legally challenged in California, the law is ambiguously worded, which means it could happen.

In short, particularly because statutes change all the time, even though most states do not have these restrictions for solicitors only, you might want to check the laws in your state before hiring an unlicensed outsider. The only outsiders I've ever heard of who are licensed *solicitors per se* without being licensed agents are affiliated with telemarketing firms.

P&C TELEPHONE SELLING USUALLY NOT "TELEMARKETING"

Sometimes P&C is sold directly over the phone, but usually the buyer rather than the seller initiates the contact, which takes the process out of the cold-calling category altogether.

FINANCIAL INSTITUTIONS TELEMARKET INSURANCE

A number of major financial institutions telemarket insurance, almost always pegging their approach on a single fairly simple lead product, frequently offering the purchaser the convenience of paying by credit card, which can be a major selling point. Oddly, an awful lot of people do not equate putting a purchase on a credit card with actually spending real money.

Sometimes these operations are in-house, but sometimes service firms handle certain components, although the principal organization usually stays very directly involved at the planning and overall supervisory levels.

TELEMARKETING OPERATIONS REGIMENTED

But whether the telephoning is in-house or through a service firm, the calls are very much the same in that the callers work from identical scripts and are expected to follow those scripts word for word. Supervision is close; expectations are clearly defined. In short, the whole process is highly regimented.

EACH SEGMENT CAN LEARN FROM THE OTHER

Yet despite the differences between most telemarketing and teleprospecting operations, much of what supports success in one is also constructively applicable to the other. The following further clarifies the differences, while also highlighting some of the similarities, between the two:

1. Unlike in teleprospecting, in insurance telemarketing, a preapproach letter is mandated by law.

2. Because only licensed insurance salespeople can legally sell insurance, if your operation hires unlicensed screeners to weed through time-wasting "suspects" in search of authentic prospects, you will need—unlike in teleprospecting, where your "product" is merely the appointment—licensed salespeople available to take over immediately for the close. If you have a national setup, make sure you are not breaking individual state laws with unlicensed initial screeners.

3. *Provided your training is thorough and your product relatively simple*, your salespeople do not need to be supersharp producers, which means you do not have to pay them anywhere near what a supersharp producer earns. Part-timers, housewives— virtually anyone with a license who is reasonably reliable and intelligent—can do the job.

4. *Provided your training is thorough and your product is relatively simple*, your screeners do not need

to be of the same caliber as a top teleprospector, either. Here, also, your labor costs can be considerably lower.

TEN TELEMARKETING RECOMMENDATIONS

Even if you are already familiar with most of the following tele*marketing* recommendations, because these operations tend to be on such a large scale, even one improvement can frequently make a substantial difference in overall profitability.

Or, if your primary interest is tele*prospecting*, then select what seems applicable to your situation and leave the rest.

1. In your preapproach mailing, always include an application blank for anyone who might be willing to buy your product by mail. Insurance sales by mail tend to "stick" better than phone sales. The decision to buy is usually less impulsive; the prospect has had more time to think it through.

   Because you will increase both your mail sales and the likelihood that prospects who have not bought by mail will nonetheless remember what you sent when you call, keep your preapproach text simple and *visual*, focusing on only one lead product. Consider a brochure rather than a letter. More often than not, when the recipient first looks at the envelope, whatever it contains is initially considered merely more "junk" mail. To be effective, words must be read. Often the right image grabs attention, making it considerably more likely that the words *will* be read. You might also consider putting something catchy—words or images—on the envelope itself.

2. Keep your product simple. Too much time spent explaining can wear out a listener who otherwise might have bought from you. As in teleprospecting, unexpected phone calls are *interrupting* whatever else the prospect had originally planned to do with the time he or she is now spending talking with you. Interruptions rarely capture the same attention span usually available in by-appointment face-to-face selling.

   Extensive explaining can also substantially raise your cost per sale. Each sale will take longer to close. Also, after you've explained, X number will still say no. The time spent on all of this could far more profitably have been spent in moving on to the next names on your list.

3. Get to the point *fast*. Small talk can lose your prospect's interest before you've even captured it.

4. Immediately, tell the prospect why they are special, why you are calling them rather than a hundred others, for example, "According to our records, you just had a baby" or "bought a house," or "We're calling everyone in your neighborhood," or "We do a lot of business with people in your line of work," or whatever. Birthdays remain a classic peg.

5. Get in as much as possible on why you're calling them and what you can do for them before you tell them your product is insurance. For example, "Hi. My name's Joe Jones. We're calling all the small-business owners in your neighborhood ('neighborhood' has a much friendlier sound than 'area') because we're offering a really unusual, excellent service—"and so on. *Then,* "I'm with XYZ Insurance, and—."

   If you are calling in connection with an *organization* in a cooperative sales effort with an insurance carrier, *mention the name of the organization before you mention the insurance company.* For example, "Hi. I'm calling *in reference to* (legally, if you are calling *from* an insurance company, you cannot say you are calling from anywhere else) the American Association of Whatever. We sent you a letter a few days ago—." This sidesteps the very common knee-jerk reaction to being solicited for insurance which inspires so many to simply growl, "Not interested," and hang up. Starting with the *organization* affiliation sets a different tone—one which may indeed make all the difference on whether your *insurance* presentation will be heard.

6. *Go for the close,* from sentence one, word one. Don't ever get sidetracked into believing any telemarketing conversation is social. Unlike face-to-face selling in which the time has been set aside for you and much of your function is to build trust through what will, it is hoped, become an ongoing personal relationship, *in telemarketing, your call is a relatively brief, oneshot connection which could be terminated without notice at any second.*

7. Never overemphasize the 30-day free-examination period. Excessive cancellations are expensive; you want sales that will stick!

8. Some of your labor will be relatively inexpensive. You'll need supervision to make sure these callers are contacting prospects rather than personal friends *and* that, when they do call prospects, they are sticking to the prepared tract, especially if there are legal constraints on what they can say.

But be careful not to create an oppressive environment. Telemarketing "sweat shops" engender excessive stress and often avoidable resentments. Both will lower productivity and increase turnover. Regular breaks, especially with a comfortable place to relax, preferably with *free* coffee/soda, tend to more than pay for themselves in their positive influence on employees' attitudes and, consequently, overall effectiveness.

9. When a sale is made, immediately ask for referrals.

10. When you send follow-up material—more detailed information laying the groundwork for a later call or confirmation of the sale and/or the policy itself—continue to sell, sell, sell! Remind your buyers of the wonderful decision they made when they bought this splendid policy. As in your initial mailing, keep it simple and visual; consider a brochure rather than a letter.

INSTITUTIONAL REGIMENTED TELE*PROSPECTING*

Although tele*prospecting* operations are rarely on the same scale as telemarketing, sometimes teleprospectors work for large insurance companies, large individual insurance agencies, or service firms of assorted sizes, where the appointments garnered are allotted to agents in an assortment of "packages." Sometimes an agency will give a new agent X number of appointments as an incentive to attract or hold the agent. In other circumstances, a producer may buy a block of time; whatever appointments are made in that time are his or hers, or perhaps there is a charge per appointment. Sponsors may supply the names and/or the script, or the client may supply either or both.

TELEPROSPECTING OFFERS MORE LEAD PRODUCT OPTIONS

Like telemarketing, this *kind* of teleprospecting generally focuses on one lead product, but because the eventual sales will emerge from face-to-face contact, there are opportunities to explain more complex packages than could reasonably be presented when the goal is to close the sale over the phone. Also, because often the primary goal in teleprospecting is merely to get in the door in hopes of subsequent, more lucrative sales, sometimes a very minor product otherwise not worth the time required to make a personal visit becomes a viable lead option.

Consequently, a broader selection of lead products is available. In Breda, Iowa, Charlene Jacobsen, manager of Breda Telemarketing, does well with slightly-off-the-beaten-path L&H products as leads, usually emphasizing a price advantage.

X-DATE CALLING

X-date calling (calling to find out when a present P&C policy expires) is becoming more and more common throughout the country, both among service firms and in individual agencies. Although having an X-date, which enables a salesperson to call the prospect at the most opportune time, does not in itself guarantee an appointment, the ultimate goal is nonetheless an appointment. If a sale materializes, it will be made in person rather than over the phone, which is what places X-date calling in the teleprospecting category.

TELEMARKETING AND INSTITUTIONAL TELEPROSPECTING SIMILARITIES

Despite the differences, the organizational teleprospecting just described is basically very much like telemarketing. As in most telemarketing operations, teleprospecting *within this framework* is usually strongly regimented. Nor do the licensed salespeople who close the sales by phone in telemarketing or those who garner appointments in teleprospecting organizations earn anywhere near what others who successfully ply these same vocations *outside* of these structures earn.

SETTING UP YOUR OWN IN-HOUSE TELEPROSPECTING OPERATION

To set up your own in-house teleprospecting operation, you need a place from which to call, relatively simple products, clear, relatively simple scripts, and enough teleprospectors to warrant paying a supervisor to stay on top of it all.

More on these issues will emerge in subsequent chapters.

INDEPENDENT TELEPROSPECTORS ARE DIFFERENT

Teleprospectors who do *not* work within this kind of structure—the individual, independent contractors directly employed by individual salespeople or sometimes by agencies but in far smaller numbers for lots more money—are a very different breed of cat, indeed! This is where I worked; it is my primary personal experience frame of reference.

INDEPENDENTS REQUIRE MORE FLEXIBLE PROCESS EVALUATION CRITERIA

Criteria for judging independents *in process* is also different. The bottom line, of course, is: are you getting the quality and quantity appointments you need?

But trying to control how this comes about by using the same criteria with independents as with monkeys-with-scripts is counterproductive, suggesting serious naivete in relation to the differences between the two groups of callers.

Unlike most independents, regimented workers are generally required to:

1. Stick tightly with whatever script they've been given.

2. Make X number, usually 20 to 30, calls per hour.

Independents work much more on their own, coming much more from their own frequently very individual styles, which often strongly influence how scripts are handled. Additionally, almost always *sophisticated independents* make far fewer calls per hour than a regimented lower-paid worker, because

1. Far more often, independents spend more time tracking down the appropriate person to speak to, as opposed to simply accepting "no" from the first person willing to listen.

2. More often, they get farther along in the presentation, with more prospects.

3. More often, they go past the basics into actual dialogue.

4. They spend more time writing up appointments, because

   a. each appointment write-up tends to be more thorough, in terms of hard data and/or personal observation—anything learned which might help you to prepare is more likely to be recorded, which cuts into time spent calling.

    b. frequently they have more appointments *to* write up.

Of course, someone goofing off on your time will also make fewer calls, but this shows up fairly quickly in the results—even more quickly, once you've developed your own guidelines on just what constitutes reasonable expectations *per* project.

SERVICE FIRMS VERSUS SHARP INDEPENDENTS—PRICE IS SIMILAR

Service firms generally charge their clients pretty much the same as a good, experienced independent teleprospector, although every now and then an independent earns— and is worth!—considerably more. Ed Lennon, in Queens, pays high school kids slightly over minimum wage to make appointments for Ed or others on his sales staff to review auto insurance. In Queens, this can get you a pretty good high school kid, but auto insurance—no matter what it may lead to—is still a low entry level.

At the opposite end of the spectrum are cold callers whose proven productivity with a far wider variety of considerably more sophisticated lead products makes them incomparably more valuable.

TOP INDEPENDENTS ARE WELL PAID—SOME ARE VERY WELL PAID!

Rayda Roundy, a licensed agent who also teleprospects six to eight hours a week for George Porter's El Camino Insurance Agency in Vista, California, works on a base rate which many independents would consider excellent as total compensation, but Rayda also receives a commission which substantially increases—sometimes even more than doubles—the base rate. *In these calls, she is strictly setting up appointments for others; she is not selling.*

BUT EVERYBODY WINS!

Other good teleprospectors in her area generally average one appointment per hour; Rayda averages one and a half to two, which helps explain why her average total hourly income is so offscale with so many others. With 50 to 100 percent more appointments, she receives a commission on 50 to 100 percent more sales. This, of course, makes everybody happy.

"If even one in four appointments results in a sale—and usually the agents here do somewhat better—then what they've paid me is negligible," she says. "So many people in this business don't understand the value of a good telephone solicitor, so they don't pay enough."

Obviously, Rayda is not going to drop her affiliation with El Camino to go read a script for a large-scale structured teleprospecting operation at an eventual maximum of slightly less than half her base rate.

INDEPENDENTS ARE GENERALLY SHARPER THAN REGIMENTED COLD CALLERS

The point is: *although occasionally there are exceptions, throughout the country those who read scripts for highly structured cold-calling operations tend to be not nearly as sharp as those who are good and work as independents.*

ORGANIZATIONAL MANAGEMENT FREQUENTLY COMPENSATES

However—point-counterpoint—many people who own or manage service firms are knock-your-socks-off smart and also have excellent backgrounds in working with a broad range of lead products. Therefore, they don't *need* super-sharp callers. Instead, through superb planning, training, and very tight control of those who work for them, their own intelligence and expertise elicits excellent results which otherwise would not be possible.

ADVANTAGES IN USING A SERVICE FIRM

Connecting with the right service firm has a lot of advantages. Although the ultimate responsibility for acquiring the appointments you need is always yours, a good service organization can free up a great deal of your time, especially from administrative chores.

It also leaves you reasonably assured of continuity. If you're counting on the appointments and the teleprospector who was getting them for you suddenly leaves, an outside firm merely brings in someone else; the tight scripts and other controls keep the people reading the scripts relatively interchangeable. Especially if you are new or haven't, for whatever reasons, had the success you seek, this can be a very viable option.

Most insurance professionals are not well trained in this area. A good service firm is not only skilled in how to hire teleprospectors who meet their needs, it can often give excellent advice on which teleprospecting approaches will probably work well *within the limitations of what is possible in a tightly scripted, regimented operation.*

ADVANTAGES IN USING INDEPENDENTS

Independents offer a far broader range of options in *what* to pursue and *at what level*. Always, the higher the entrance level you are aiming for, the more important the proficiency of your teleprospectors.

Nor is there any question that a good independent teleprospector can get you appointments which would fall through the cracks in a superstructured environment, even at lower levels, especially if you have a particularly difficult target group or perhaps a relatively complex lead product or anything else that may require go-with-the-flow fast flexible thinking.

"Oh, I don't own any insurance," a small-business owner once told me. "Don't believe in it."

"Hey, terrific!" I responded. "No guts, no glory, right?"

He laughed. I laughed. I got the appointment.

This is *not* a scripted scenario!

An independent also allows you to "test market" new approaches on a far smaller scale. Usually, you can get an *idea* of how it's going in about four hours—sometimes less. Or perhaps your overall immediate ambitions are to set up only one or two people for one or two days—or fewer—per week. Very few service firms are interested in anything this small scale.

PRIMARY PROBLEMS IN HIRING AND WORKING WITH INDEPENDENTS

In virtually all cases, the primary problems in hiring and training independents emanate from agents' own lack of good teleprospecting training. You cannot show someone else how to do something you don't really understand yourself.

The training most agents receive on how to hire, train, and work with independents is usually even more deficient.

SELECTING A SERVICE FIRM

Some service firms are excellent. All those mentioned in this book were highly recommended by the particular agents who referred me to them.

But some leave much to be desired, and virtually all—good, bad, or indifferent—want a sizable commitment from you before they begin to work with you. Therefore, you need to be cautious. If you pick one which does not specialize in insurance, will it do well for an insurance client? And if it *does* specialize in insurance, *how does it set its boundaries between clients?* For example, will the firm solicit for you in the particular ZIP Code or profession or whatever other category especially interests you, or will you have to settle for what some other producer did not want? Especially if you do not live in a large city where an abundance of names in just about any category is available, this can be a major concern. *With your own teleprospector, your only limits on where you can call are those you set.*

VISIT THE PHYSICAL FACILITY

If you do decide to use a service firm, visit the firm's physical facility. If possible, take along someone whose judgment you respect. Talk to some of their clients and also to some of their teleprospectors. Ask how many appointments they normally get in an hour and what kind of appointments. Certain kinds are relatively easy, for example, auto insurance, while life can be *very* difficult.

Most of the good producers I've known over the years were smart, but also intuitive. Perhaps the intuition was there to begin with, or perhaps it grew to meet the challenges of this particular business, but wherever it came from, it's one of the most important assets you have in selecting an outside firm. This is why it's especially important to do your investigating in person. Somebody who is knock-your-socks-off smart may very well influence what you *think*, but before you sign anything, see how you *feel*!

A FIRM NOT NEAR YOU MAY BE OKAY

If there are no firms in your immediate vicinity, it will probably help you to know that growing numbers call all over the country. If you belong to a professional association, perhaps they can direct you to one that is reputable and calls in your area, even if located across the country.

IF YOU'VE DECIDED TO DO IT YOURSELF OR TO HIRE AN INDEPENDENT

However, perhaps you're not seriously considering an outside operation. Perhaps, instead, you've pretty much decided to either do your own calling or to hire an independent.

More on these issues—doing your own calling as opposed to hiring an independent—will be explored in Chapter 5. *How* to hire, train, and evaluate an outsider is covered in Chapter 6.

5

Maximizing Your Personal Calling Potential—or Hire Someone Else?

APPOINTMENTS/INSURANCE—DIFFERENT SELLING SKILLS REQUIRED

Tele*prospecting*—selling *appointments* to sell insurance— is very different from selling *insurance*. Appointments and insurance are different products, *requiring different selling skills.*

When you "sell" an appointment, your "product" *is* the appointment. Your "close" takes place when the prospect agrees to meet with you. In the strict context of teleprospecting, the *appointment is made over the phone*; the *insurance sale evolves from subsequent face-to-face contact.*

DO YOUR OWN CALLING?

Sometimes people who are good at selling insurance are also good at selling appointments. However, if telephone cold calling is your primary prospecting vehicle and you are *not* good at it, you have two alternatives. You can

1. Become good
2. Hire someone else to do it for you

To become good—or better—a lot of what you'll need, you can learn. Most of the rest is attitude, which can be changed. But the balance—what divides success from super-success—you either have or you don't; it's talent. Yet I've seen far less talented teleprospectors do much better than some with lots more talent *when those with less talent were better prepared.*

If you intend to do your own calling, as opposed to hiring someone else, it is probably for one or more of the following reasons, presented in no particular order of importance.

1. You feel it builds a more personal relationship with potential clients much sooner.
2. It enables you to qualify a prospect subtly in ways most outsiders never could, to decide well in advance whether or not you really want a particular appointment.
3. It preserves continuity in cases where follow-up calls are needed to "close" the appointment (outside teleprospectors are not known for their longevity in any one particular job).
4. It allows you more flexibility on callbacks. Outsiders are usually available only for set hours on set days, which may not jibe with a particular prospect's availability.
5. It allows you to switch pitches in midstream. If a prospect is willing to dialogue with you but your lead product is not catching his or her interest,

you can immediately draw from expertise on other products which an outsider will not have, thereby sometimes salvaging the potential appointment.

6. It enables you to refine your total calling process more quickly, without relying on feedback from someone else whose input may or may not be on target.

7. Although you'd rather hire someone else, laying out the upfront money would be difficult.

8. The quantity of calling needed is insufficient to interest a service firm, and you believe the effort required to hire, train, and work with an independent for only a very few hours per week is, in conjunction with other considerations, not worth the investment.

9. You've given up on finding anyone other than yourself who would do an even halfway decent job for you.

10. Fill in the blank. Why do you handle your own calling? Whatever your answers, the process of thinking them through will help you to either reaffirm with new clarity why you operate as you do or to consider seriously alternatives which may, in fact, substantially improve your overall productivity.

OBSTACLES TO HIRING OUTSIDERS SURMOUNTABLE

But perhaps your first choice is to hire someone else. If so, the good news is, number 7—laying out upfront money—and number 9—difficulty in finding a good outsider—are surmountable. Not only can this book help you to earn more money, it can also help you manage far more effectively those resources you already have.

And in *most* geographical areas, if you know *how* and are willing to pay appropriately, finding good outsiders is easier than you probably realize, all of which is addressed in the next chapter.

REASONS TO HIRE OUTSIDERS

If your first choice is to hire someone else, probably it is because

1. You believe your time is more productively spent elsewhere.
2. Even though you've done everything reasonably possible to improve, you're still not good.
3. For whatever other reasons, you believe an outsider will probably do a better job than you could/would do for yourself.
4. Teleprospecting makes you nuts. You *hate* it.

HONOR THE FEELING FACTOR

Point 4 is as valid as any other. If these are your feelings, farming it out in no way diminishes you. Instead, it suggests you have the sense to reduce stress in your life wherever you reasonably can. Certainly you are not alone if teleprospecting pressures in general, and rejections in particular, sometimes get to you. If so, but a walk around the block renews you, fine.

However, if your confidence is being eroded, leaving you with self-doubts—especially if you sometimes carry these doubts into your next phone call or, worse, into your next appointment—it may help to remember that the capacity to deal with rejection this intensive is another area where the abilities required to teleprospect successfully are not necessarily the same as those required to sell insurance.

Of course, with awareness and a number of other tools (see Chapter 14), feelings can change.

In the meantime, if this last point is a serious issue for you, recognizing and accepting it as such will enable you to

1. Work on your feelings

2. For the moment, accept them, allowing them appropriate weight in your final decision on whether to hire someone else.

BURNOUT POINT

Sometimes working on feelings related to teleprospecting will facilitate a major transformation after which you can call and call on into the sunset, and not mind at all. However, in my own experience and also according to virtually all of the people I've discussed it with, there is what I call a burnout point, which varies widely from individual to individual.

"I generally call for an hour at most," says Ned Burns, an agent with the MDS Insurance Group in Rockford, Illinois. "After that, I burn out."

"Two hours at most, one is better," says Craig Beachnaw, LIC, an 18-year producer in Lansing, Michigan.

"I generally have enough prospects where I could call for eight hours at a stretch, for three or four days in a row. However, I cannot maintain the pace."

Whatever your burnout point, if you're getting what you need within that time frame, no problem. Or perhaps you gauge your results by *number of appointments per number of calls*. This is most common among agents, while most *outsiders* use a *per hour* standard, probably because most outsiders are paid an hourly base rate.

However, no matter what measurement you use, *are* you reasonably satisfied with your telephone cold-calling results?

And "should" you be? What's your criterion? Where did it originate? *Is it valid*? How can you know?

ESTABLISHING REASONABLE PERFORMANCE STANDARDS

Establishing reasonable performance standards can be difficult. A number of producers I've known over the years—and quite a few in other states whom I talked with while researching this book—clearly (at least, clear to me) were not operating at anywhere near their potential.

And yet, they were successful—sometimes, to some degree.

And because sometimes, to some degree, they were successful, most had no idea there was anything "wrong," that they *could* have been much better.

This is a perplexing issue. If your standards are too low, you'll be satisfied too easily, allowing valuable potential appointments to slip through your fingers, but if your standards are too high, you're setting yourself up to *never* feel satisfied, and that doesn't work, either. All of us need moments in which we can look in a mirror, and say, "Hey—nice job, well done!"

So, how can you be sure you're doing well, as opposed to just *thinking* you are, only because you don't know any better?

MISSING: UNIVERSAL YARDSTICKS

Because there are no universal yardsticks against which to measure results by individual producers teleprospecting on individual projects in different parts of the country, there are no universal answers.

Stated in a more personal context, if what you're doing is virtually identical to what someone else is doing, but he or she is doing it in May and you're doing it one week before Christmas, or he or she is doing it in a depressed coal-mining community in West Virginia while you're doing it in an affluent section of Connecticut, comparisons mean very little.

There *is* hard data on this, but unfortunately, it is generally not really helpful *to individual agents doing their own calling* because

1. Not even *most* of the variables have been taken into consideration.

2. *Most of it comes from teleprospecting firms, which, as explained in the last chapter, usually constitute a whole different ball game from agents doing their own calling.*

NO VALID ACROSS-THE-BOARD INDUSTRYWIDE STANDARDS

Joni Fairbrother is an instructor employed by the Independent Agents and Brokers of Arizona; she teaches teleprospecting throughout the state.

"For every good call you make," she says, "you'll get between 15 and 20 'no's.' The usual hit rate is 1 in 20, unless you're doing X-date calling. Then, you can double or even triple it. With X-dates, out of 20 calls, expect 3 or 4."

If I were pushed to the edge of a cliff and forced to name numbers, I'd have to admit Joni is on target, in sync with the industry myth that such a number exists. Indeed, the myth says, *about* 1 in 20, with it's time-based counterpart of 1 per hour.

Yet every producer and independent teleprospector I talked to had their own numbers, some as low as 1 in 20 calls (Joni's figures), or even less, but some as high as 7 or 8 in only *10* calls, on an ongoing basis, some with a product as difficult as straight personal life, which many perfectly respectable valid industry authorities have flatly, *publicly* and repeatedly stated is absolutely impossible as a teleprospecting lead product.

UNIVERSAL STANDARDS ARE NOT IMPORTANT—UNDERSTANDING IS

This is not intended to confuse or to discourage you; you don't *need* a universal standard.

What you need is to *understand each component, and how it fits into the overall process.* This will enable you to sit down with a sophistication you've never before experienced and put together assorted "packages" from which your own performance standards will emerge. Certain projects, if well handled, should indeed net you 1 appointment in 20 calls, but others should, because of how all the variables come together, do considerably better—or worse!

With understanding, your diagnostic skills will improve substantially. If a new calling venture is not working, why? If it's fixable, how? Once it *is* fixed, how can you make it even better?

And you will become considerably more effective at bringing out the best in anyone you hire to call for you.

DIFFERENCES BETWEEN A REFERRAL AND A COLD CALL

In establishing reasonable expectations for yourself and/or others who report to you, it's important to understand that there are *degrees* of cold calling, some more likely than others to be productive, although any can provide the lead you need for your next major sale.

The warmest and usually best are referrals. Craig Beachnaw, in Lansing, Michigan, generally calls only on referrals now, yet still finds it draining. Not as warm, but not completely freezing, are prospects who have been approached first by mail (covered in Chapter 9).

Through a referral, you enter the picture with at least some measure of credibility. Yet even without a direct referral, or preapproach letter, if you live in a relatively small defined community in which your reputation or that of your agency precedes you, your approach is still not completely cold.

ICE-COLD CALLS

Ice-cold calls are to complete strangers. With ice-cold calls, you are the new kid in town—unknown, untested. Sometimes the natives are friendly, but sometimes definitely restless. You'll need to prove yourself; you'll need much more patience than is usually required in a warmer calling climate.

"DECISION MAKERS ONLY!"

Just how cold your approach is, is sometimes reflected in how far up the ladder you'll be able to start. Although certainly no one wants to waste time making presentations to high school kids who are only there filing papers for the summer, sometimes a conversation/appointment with the decision maker is something a salesperson coming in through a *cold-call* must earn; there's no way around it. Sometimes the only route to the comptroller really is through the bookkeeper, the route to the owner through the comptroller. *Part of what they're paid for is to screen you, and they're not going to budge.*

To insist on more from yourself—or your teleprospector, if you've hired an outsider—is not reasonable.

But neither is it reasonable to assume that going through a screener—or two—means you won't ever get to the person you wanted to see in the first place who may, indeed, become not only a client, but eventually a nice, warm referral source!

None of this is intended to suggest that you cannot make a solid appointment with the top person immediately, through teleprospecting. You absolutely can. The point is, if you *limit* yourself *only* to immediate appointments with top people, you will miss some superb opportunities. *And sometimes you will also miss critically important chances to gain support from powerful, key underlings before you lay it all out for the top man / woman, who will ask their opinion as soon as you're out the door!*

QUALIFYING TELEPHONE COLD-CALL APPOINTMENTS

When you make an appointment, quite reasonably you want it to be with someone ready, willing, and able to buy what you're selling. But decision maker or not, if only you could know which organizations and/or family units *were* ready, willing, and able, obviously you could save a great deal of time.

However, trying to qualify too much too soon in a teleprospecting call can be as big a mistake as beginning a sale prematurely, which will be discussed in depth later in this chapter.

When working from a referral, you are a stranger; in an *ice-cold* call, you are a *complete* stranger. Immediately requesting heavy financial information can easily offend.

Also remember, your call is an interruption. Even to set a time to call back to pursue this information, *which the prospect will probably quite readily give you, as the face-to-face sale progresses,* is playing brinkmanship with what might otherwise have been an excellent appointment.

This is not to suggest that if the product with which you caught the prospect's interest is, for example, of value only to companies with 25 or fewer employees that you can't ask whether his or her business meets this criterion. Or perhaps you're doing pension design, and to prepare for the meeting, you need to know what kind of pension they already have.

Of course, if you connect with someone obviously eager to tell you everything you could ever possibly want to know, nothing here is intended to suggest you cut it short!

GUIDELINES FOR QUALIFYING APPOINTMENTS IN FIRST PHONE CALL

If any of this seems confusing, it doesn't have to be. Because different situations come up so quickly, you won't always have time to think clearly in the immediate instant. Therefore, *guidelines*—thought through when you *did* have time—can be a valuable investment.

For reasons already given plus others discussed later in this chapter, your safest approach in qualifying

teleprospected appointments is: Don't push; keep it lean
and clean, with absolutely clear boundaries at all times
between what you *need* from the prospect, as opposed to
what you merely *want.*

SECURITIES AND INSURANCE
TELEPROSPECTORS NOT INTERCHANGEABLE!

Relevant to this issue, many insurance and securities'
professionals search each other's ranks in pursuit of good
teleprospectors, in the mistaken belief that the two kinds
of cold calling are much more alike than they really are.

There are big differences. Among them, securities
salespeople hire far fewer outside callers; far more often
securities salespeople make their own contacts, their
strength in their product sophistication and general sales
skills *rather than* telephone skills per se. Also, standard
telephone cold-call *immediate* qualifying techniques for
securities analysts can very much offend the wrong insurance prospect, while the lower-key approach common to so
many successful insurance professionals can be inadequate for securities' professionals.

On the subject of solidifying *insurance* cold-call
appointments, indeed, less is usually more!

PRE-APPOINTMENT SALES EFFORTS OFTEN
UNDERMINE SUCCESS

Another pitfall through which even seasoned professionals often undermine potential success is failure to realize
that tele*prospecting* is not tele*marketing.*

Because unlicensed outsiders are not legally per-
mitted to sell insurance, this is a major issue for agents
only.

With few exceptions, which will be addressed later in this chapter, agents who attempt to *market* during a tele*prospecting* call place themselves at a significant disadvantage. Cold-call connections are, at best, tenuous. If you begin selling to a prospect who may have to hang up virtually without notice, even if you do get a chance to pick up on it again, your presentation will have become segmented, fragmented. You can irretrievably lose your timing, your continuity—in short, the incrementally built final punch which so often tips a would-be sale one way or the other.

But that's only part of the dilemma.

BIG DIFFERENCES BETWEEN TELEPHONE AND FACE-TO-FACE CONTACT

"Communication by phone is very limited," says Mike Axton, an L&H salesman for the last eight years in Laurel, Mississippi. Today, virtually all of his business is through referrals. However, he adds, even when the initial telephone contact is referral based, "You don't have their full attention."

Nor can you reasonably expect it, even with a referral. A *cold* call is more difficult. Cold calls are *always* interruptions; listening to you was not in Mr. Prospect's schedule. If you're going to end up with a sale, you need to catch interest quickly, not try to hold it too long, and keep your eye on the *immediate* goal, which is the *appointment*. In the face-to-face contact of a scheduled appointment, using time which has been blocked out on both sides for this purpose, you are on much more solid ground!

With only a telephone cold call, particularly in fast, competitive cities, while Mr. Prospect is talking to you, most likely another phone is ringing, his secretary has something for him to sign, someone else has just entered his office, and, especially if we're dealing with New York, quite possibly he's also swatting at a cockroach.

But even if you live in an area where life generally moves more slowly—or wherever you are, if you get lucky and simply catch someone at the right mellow moment—phone calls still can be cut short. Or prospects who seemed seriously interested—eager to hear more from you—may abruptly back off; often you will never know why.

PLAY IT SAFE—MAKE THE APPOINTMENT!

You do not need to risk any of this. *Make your appointment*; that's what the call is about. In most of the appointments I've made, there is a particular instant in which the timing is right, the chemistry is right, and you *either* close, or like water when something has been thrown into it, the moment that was open a second before closes; the opportunity is gone. *Maybe* you'll get another crack at it, but more often than not, you won't.

GEOGRAPHICAL DIFFERENCES INFLUENCE APPROACH—GOAL IS THE SAME

In different parts of the country, different *styles* dominate. Some are laid back, even gentle, far less direct; others much more sharply focused and assertive. Certainly you need to pace yourself in harmony with your own area, but the bottom line remains the same. *Most agents who are also successful teleprospectors stay clear on what they are calling about*; they know it is not about selling insurance—*yet. It is about setting appointments*, arranging to get in the door to start building the *face-to-face* personal relationships on which their ultimate success depends for present, add-on, and future referral business. Some of the many I spoke to had learned it by trial and error, others through managers, the experiences of colleagues, and/or assorted forms of professionally prepared sales material, over the years.

ADDITIONAL DISADVANTAGES IN STARTING AN ACTUAL SALE BY PHONE

In addition, Mike Axton adds, "Over the phone, you can't *show* them anything."

Dorothy Scott, also in Laurel, Mississippi, goes even further in emphasizing the significance of visual communication. "Body language gives major clues on where people are coming from," she says. "I'm much more comfortable face to face. Eye contact can be more important than words. I don't like telephone cold calling; I usually do better if I just drop in."

But even when she drops in, *she is not yet trying to sell insurance.* Instead, *she is seeking an appointment,* a *scheduled* block of time when she can have the prospect's *full* attention.

EXCEPTIONS

Anyone can come across a prospect who doggedly will not go any farther than the phone call without sales information beyond what a producer might want—or an outsider be able—to give over the phone in a cold call. When this happens, I recommend you go with the flow. Give as much information as necessary, but remember: your goal is still the appointment.

Prospects with this mind-set are why backup salespeople for outside teleprospectors can be important; how important depends, of course, on the relative potential value of each appointment.

ENHANCING YOUR PERSONAL TELEPHONE SKILLS

The balance of this chapter focuses on enhancing your personal telephone skills. Even if you are not planning to do your own calling, what follows will help you to supervise/work with others far more effectively.

MAXIMIZING YOUR ONLY TELEPHONE SENSORY TOOL—SOUND!

When you use a telephone, you have only one source of sensory input/output: *sound! There is a lot you can do with sound.*

How's your voice? Animated? Clear? Friendly? Well modulated? My tendency is to talk too fast; slowing down is a conscious process. A young woman I trained needed consciously to lower her voice; otherwise, *over the phone* she sounded too childlike to be taken seriously. Do you come over nervous, or at the opposite end of the spectrum, as though you're completely at home with every word? Remember, from the prospect's point of view, the issue is not what you *do* feel, it's only how you *sound.*

ADVANTAGES IN SOUNDING LIKE THE PROSPECTS YOU CALL

Do you have an accent? If so, is it a plus or minus within the particular group you want to approach? This can be a foreign or regional American accent. The garment district in New York City is dominated by people with "New York" accents, while the speech of people in advertising agencies is generally closer to the national stereotype associated with Ivy League educations.

Although it's not *essential* to sound like the people you call, if you do, usually you can build trust faster. You will also meet with less resistance from screeners. They will be far more likely to assume—simply because of how you sound—that your business with whoever you want to talk to—*who sounds like you*—is legitimate.

CHECK OUT YOUR VOICE

You might want to tape record your voice. Simply speak into the machine, or—even better—record your end of some cold calls. Play it back later, when you're relatively relaxed. What do you like and dislike? Input from others can be especially valuable.

If you're not satisfied with what you hear, usually a voice coach can help. If your town has a theater company, probably some of the actors can steer you in the right direction. Radio station announcers usually have voice training; they, also, can be an effective referral source. Simply call and ask. Or run a newspaper ad. Another option (although rarely as good as personal contact coaching) is audio training tapes.

Especially if you do your own calling, this is not something to do when you "have time." It is an immediate priority.

MULTILEVEL LISTENING

Also in teleprospecting, as opposed to face-to-face selling, your only *input* is sound. Usually I can tell very early in the conversation whether or not a "sale" is likely. Content is a factor, but *what I hear in other people's timing* is often more significant. If I'm braced for the next objection, but they hesitate, this tells me they are probably weighing what I've said. Now I know what to say next.

Breathing can be especially revealing. Listen to your own breathing; get in touch with how different it is when you are irritated as opposed to when you are comfortably in sync with what's going on around you. How are you breathing right now? What does it tell you?

Breathing can tell me prospects are not listening—they have drawn a breath to say what's already on their minds before I've finished my sentence—or it can tell me they *are* listening—and wavering on just how much more time they'll give me, which defines *my* timing on when to expand an idea as opposed to zeroing in on the close.

MATCHING YOUR PROSPECT'S STYLE

You can also use what you *hear* to match your prospect's style, thereby helping the prospect to feel comfortable with—more receptive to—you. Some of this relates to content, but much doesn't.

When you first connect, you have little to work with in terms of matching, because you are doing most of the talking. You are introducing yourself and your product. However, as soon as you get a reaction, you can begin adjusting. Is their overall speech pattern fast or slow? Are they formal? If so, I'll put a subtle distance between us, acknowledging their space. Are they rushed, or laid back—or perhaps flip? Match it; *blend with their style.*

Blending encompasses

1. voice tone, including volume
2. pacing
3. attitude

Practicing this is so easy, it will probably surprise you. Basically, all you need is to *become aware of it*. Notice *yourself and others* in both social and business conversations. Tune in. Who's matching who?

"Matching" or "blending," you will soon realize, is common. It's perfectly normal. *Probably you are already doing it*, sometimes, to one degree or another, without even realizing it, as others are already doing it, sometimes, with you!

The difference in *teleprospecting* matching is, *initially*, you *deliberately* allow the *prospect* to set the pace and style. Later, as the relationship becomes more multi-dimensional, your own style may indeed take the lead, but by then you can afford it; by then, you'll have a connection far more solid than anything you might reasonably hope for in a single hit-or-miss teleprospecting call.

STAY TUNED FOR NEXT CHAPTER!

Much of the material you have just read, although focused on doing your own calling, also would be valuable to you in relating to an independent. Equally so, much of what is covered in the next two chapters will be helpful even if you are not anticipating using anyone else.

CHAPTER 6

"Collision Insurance"— Establishing Independent Teleprospector Boundaries

INDEPENDENT TELEPROSPECTORS: THE SUBJECT OF THIS CHAPTER

Throughout this chapter, unless otherwise specified, the subject is not teleprospecting operations in which, basically, a closely supervised group reads identical scripts prepared by others.

The focus is on "independents," one or more sharp, well-paid individuals brought in by one or more salespeople to teleprospect on highly personalized projects.

IN PARTNERSHIPS, TELEPROSPECTORS NEED ONE CLEAR "BOSS"

Most issues relative to working with a partner are covered in the next chapter. However, "collision insurance" needs your attention if you and a partner together hire one independent teleprospector. Although certainly both of you would be in frequent direct contact with the caller, it's important that the two of you not run into each other and *over* the teleprospector. To avoid this, either you or your partner needs to become the designated "administrator." *Only* the administrator assigns specific calling tasks, sets working hours, makes payment, and defines how appointments are to be handled, for example, how much qualifying is to be done over the phone; are appointments to be set in one name, or both; or whatever else comes up.

REDUCING DEPENDENCY ON INDEPENDENTS

With or without a partner, if you are an insurance agent who is also good at "selling appointments" by phone, to institute/continue your own calling as you break in an independent can serve as backup, a bridge to keep your new appointment flow moving smoothly while you gradually turn over more and more responsibility to your independent.

But whether or not you do any of your own calling, your involvement remains critical, especially in the beginning as the independent becomes acclimated to your style and needs. With a *new project*, this is even more important, not so much because the teleprospector needs *you*, but because you need to understand/master your *process*.

MOST TELEPROSPECTORS ARE TRANSITORY

Most teleprospectors are transitory. Almost always, telephone soliciting is "plan B"; it's what they do for money while waiting for what they really want to materialize.

If you don't master your process, you are vulnerable to making yourself nuts hiring and training one independent after another, each time hoping that this time you'll get what you need without quite as many trial and error mishaps as last time. The legendary transience of independents is one of the biggest selling points used by service firms.

CONTINUITY THROUGH PROCESS CONTROL

But once you own your process, you're not nearly as vulnerable as you are otherwise. When you know what works, training someone new becomes relatively automatic. No more, "Gosh, Joe got all those appointments for me, but then he went away!"

You won't *need* Joe. Granted, his replacement may not be quite as good *in some areas*, but if you know how to hire, train, and evaluate, you'll find that in other areas, the replacement probably makes up for it quite adequately.

RULES AND GUIDELINES—THE DEFINITE DIFFERENCE

There's a definite difference between a *rule* and a guideline. It's a rule that you don't dispose of your competitors by poisoning them, a guideline that if you want to get from Queensboro Plaza to Grand Central Station, you take the #7 subway train. You *could* take the N train, then change at 59th, or the Q32 bus or a cab, or limo, or any number of other perfectly viable alternatives. It's your choice, as long as it fits your *guidelines*. Guidelines are *options* on how to *get where you want to go*.

Most teleprospecting *process* control is about guidelines. The fact that independents are generally more successful if you use guidelines rather than strict rules is another area where regimented solicitors part company with independents.

INDEPENDENTS ARE NOT "MONKEYS-WITH-SCRIPTS"

Independents are *not* monkeys-with-scripts. When a monkey-with-a-script is not working out, usually the monkey, not the script, is replaced.

Sometimes, indeed, independents need to be replaced. But if you've done your hiring carefully, usually it pays to be more patient before deciding you've made a mistake.

ALL INDEPENDENTS ARE NOT CREATED EQUAL

Because independents are often very different from each other, it's important never to be so locked into expectations based on other experiences that you can't make room for variations. Especially in sophisticated operations aimed at getting you in at a higher level, what worked well for one teleprospector may not work at all for another.

REFINING, RESHAPING TO MAXIMIZE RESOURCES

When this happens—teleprospector A was terrific with certain material, while teleprospector B can't get it off the ground—often merely reshaping your telephone presentation to suit your new caller's style solves the problem.

However, sometimes more is necessary. Sometimes going with the flow may carry you considerably further from your original plans than you ever expected, but so what? The bottom line remains, you're getting what you need; the process is working!

In Charleston, South Carolina, Thomas Masi, an agent with the Shirley Merrill Agency, recently brought in an independent.

"We wanted local businesses with 25 or more employees," Tom explains, "but the man we hired is so good with smaller organizations, 7 to 15, we're keeping him. This has become what we're concentrating on; the mom and pop operations. It's working very well."

This is not a recommendation that you reshape your original goals to accommodate whatever calling talent lands on your doorstep. It merely means that *sometimes*—if it meets your needs, if it comes together in a way that works for you—it is a valid option.

LISTEN TO YOUR CALLERS

If you're doing your own calling, you'll pick up a lot of *process*-related information. This works, this doesn't. But if you're not doing your own, you will pick up this *kind* of information only if you *listen* to the person/people you have hired. Take the time!

Ask questions, too, and never underestimate the value of those which are open end, for example, "Any problems? Why do you think it went so well *or* went so poorly? Anything you feel I can help you with? *Any suggestions?*"

By asking questions of this nature, and *genuinely listening* to the answers, you not only enhance your immediate data base; you also help establish a climate in which ongoing joint creative improvement on the overall project is far more likely to flourish.

In an operation already off and running, new ideas usually can be tested in relatively few calls; your "research" investment is generally minimal.

BUT KEEP AND RESPECT HISTORICAL DATA

However, with all due respect for flexibility and creativity, it's also important that you keep and appreciate historical data.

Over the years, I've met very few insurance agents—especially among the really good ones—who enjoyed anything even remotely clerical in nature. Collecting and maintaining historical data definitely requires a clerical investment. Nonetheless, if you do not keep careful records of "packages" that work, you doom yourself to wasting a lot of time retracing ground already covered.

The right records will remind you or introduce a newcomer to the fact that this particular approach/product *when properly presented* to this market has a history of netting, ballpark, X number of appointments in X number of calling hours. Although products/approaches/styles change, your file will nonetheless remain a resource, a square marked "go" from which to continually update, enhance, and evaluate both your independent teleprospector and your overall process.

For more on structuring these packages, *which does not need to be either complicated or particularly time consuming*, see Chapter 11, which deals with systems/clerical backup.

WHY CALLING TERRITORY BOUNDARIES ARE ESSENTIAL

Simply stated, teleprospecting boundaries define the parameters of who's calling whom and what happens with the results.

When agents simply compete with each other or when individual teleprospectors *who do all the cold calling for one agent only* pick up the phone, boundaries are not an issue. However, it's not always that elementary.

To *share* your teleprospecting with an independent successfully, and/or to share one or more teleprospectors with other salespeople in or out of the same office successfully, clear upfront boundaries are absolutely vital. Without them, the results—embarrassing overlap, confusion, conflicts of interest, and not infrequently major league resentments—quite commonly reflect more problems than solutions!

WARNING: INTERSECTION AHEAD

Calling responsibilities can be divided in many ways. If you're using only one independent who is working only for you, anything that suits both of you is fine. Or if you share one teleprospector with one partner, with either you or your partner clearly the designated administrator, and the teleprospector works only for the two of you, the situation is still basically simple. With only two or three cars on the road, all observing the speed limit, the likelihood of a collision is small.

But once that caller is working for even one other agent *in or out of your office*, who is *competing with you*, it gets infinitely more complex. When the *same* teleprospector ends up talking to the *same* prospect on behalf of two (or more!) *competing* agents, *that* is a collision!

ANATOMY OF A CRASH!

If the teleprospector is, for example, calling pharmacies, so salesperson A can present virtually every insurance product imaginable, obviously that same teleprospector cannot reasonably call pharmacies for salesperson B, *unless* the pharmacies for salesperson A are in only one *town* or perhaps one particular *ZIP Code* and in another town or ZIP Code for B. Or perhaps the teleprospector works with certain letters in the alphabet for A, others for B.

If you've managed to follow all this so far, hang on; it gets even more interesting.

Suppose agent A is targeting pharmacies, while agent B is not targeting pharmacies at all. No conflict, right? Not quite! Suppose B is targeting small businesses in the same general area as the pharmacies, with a number-of-employees range that fits many of the pharmacies, while agent *C* is targeting health clubs, which of course are also small businesses and, consequently, overlap with the best interests of agent B.

Or suppose agent A is leading with discounted *personal* coverage offered to members of a professional association, while agent B is leading with *business* tax savings, to exactly the same group.

Or suppose *both* agents—with the same or with competing offices—have hired the same teleprospector to call the same prospects, using as a door-opener the superiority of the agency.

Now add a second teleprospector, now a third, now more; now let's throw more agents into the stew, with care not to oversimplify by underestimating the quantity of

potential lead products which could fall all over each other
so very easily.

In short, C-R-A-S-H!

STEADY, STABLE, AND ALL
YOURS—SOMETIMES

Ideally, teleprospectors who work for you will work *only*
for you; sometimes this happens. *Occasionally,* a
teleprospector will remain with the same agent for years!

Nor is the experimentation discussed throughout
this chapter appropriate for everyone. Many salespeo-
ple/agencies in many parts of the country have excellent
reputations in their particular area of expertise, which
keeps them sufficiently busy; they are not interested in
conquering new horizons. In these environments, relationships between agents and teleprospectors are often exceptionally stable.

EXCEPTIONALLY STABLE
TELEPROSPECTOR/SALESPERSON
RELATIONSHIPS

The teleprospector might even be "family," someone employed by the salesperson/agency in some other capacity,
who occasionally simply gets on the phone and does a nice
job. Often in small agencies in small towns, the
"teleprospector" is the producer's secretary, when she has
a spare moment. On a larger scale, in Tacoma, Washington, Judy Peterson, a longtime customer service rep with
Tom Taylor Insurance Brokers, Inc., picks up the phone
for about an hour each day. She follows up on P&C X-
dates, using as a lead the quality of her agency, which she
knows so well. Meanwhile, four hours away in the small

town of Richland, Karen Fruchtl, *formerly* in customer service with the Spencer Kinney Agency, now teleprospects full time for that agency. Like Judy in Tacoma, Karen is "family." Her approach? The quality of her agency!

But these are exceptional situations. Far more commonly, to avoid crashes, managers/producers must deal very clearly with hiring, training, and boundaries!

ZIP CODES ARE COMMON BOUNDARY; OTHER OPTIONS ARE AVAILABLE

ZIP Codes are probably the most common boundaries used by service firms *which have clients in direct competition with each other.* However, this evolved because it meets the needs of the service firm, not necessarily because it's best for you. Sometimes it may indeed be best, but when working with independents, your range of options is considerably wider.

EXERCISING OTHER OPTIONS

When working with independents, you can define boundaries that suit *you,* then work only with callers who agree to respect these boundaries; for example, this month, you want appointments with local small businesses, focusing on pension design as a door-opener. Your category is: *Geographical, Small-Business Pensions.* In bringing in an outsider, you will use only someone *who works according to geographic boundaries* and is not already soliciting your calling area for someone else, in the small-business category *or any other which might compete with it.*

Whoever you hire must understand this immediately; while they work for you, certainly they are free to also work for others, but they must observe with the others whatever boundary form they agreed to with you.

SWITCHING CATEGORIES

However, perhaps once you've got all that in order, the following month, you'll decide you'd rather concentrate on a particular profession, for example, chiropractors, but to find enough, you must include in addition to your own town, five neighboring towns. Your *category* becomes *Profession, Chiropractor.* Now, you need someone who calls *by profession.* Geography is no longer the boundary.

Is your teleprospector willing and in a position to switch the *nature* of his or her calling boundaries from *Geographic, Small-Business Pensions,* to *Professions, Chiropractors?*

Often, this will be easy. Perhaps you're the only person the teleprospector is working for, or perhaps his or her other employers will comfortably accommodate.

However, if you can*not* arrange to have their boundary category changed—if, perhaps, they are locked into it by commitments on this basis to other salespeople—then hire someone else.

GOOD TELEPROSPECTORS USUALLY FIND NEW WORK QUICKLY

If switching from one to another teleprospector this readily seems capricious in relation to the teleprospectors, it's not. If they're good (and if they're not, you wouldn't keep them long, anyway) in most cases, they'll have no problem finding others to hire them within their existing boundaries framework. All I had to do to pick up new clients was talk to enough people in suits —male or female—while waiting for elevators outside any large insurance agency where I already had a client.

And then, of course, there's always the Yellow Pages, under Insurance.

THE "FAIRNESS FACTOR"—WHO GETS THE GOOD APPOINTMENTS?

Another serious boundary issue often rears its ugly head when a common pool of appointments is parceled out among two or more salespeople. Because one longer session is generally more productive than two short, occasionally two producers who are not partners will share the same teleprospector, *dividing the appointments between them*, but often considerably more than two salespeople and one teleprospector are involved. Perhaps the pool was set up by individual salespeople, or perhaps it is agency sponsored, a full-scale ongoing in-house operation.

In any of these circumstances, the question of who will end up with the *good* appointments is, at best, difficult. At worst, it's explosive. The anecdote related in Chapter 1, in which the dust is still settling from the producer who funneled appointments—after he had skimmed the cream for himself—powerfully illustrates the dangers inherent in having appointments "funneled" at all. Even if your process seems foolproof against complaints, somebody somewhere within that process is going to have a great deal of power. Indeed, who gets the good appointments? The possibilities for unfairness—and/or for *perceived* unfairness, *which can be just as destructive—* need to be taken very seriously.

ROTATION: AN ALTERNATIVE IN PARCELING OUT APPOINTMENTS

Sometimes appointments are sequentially rotated: within a defined calling period, the first goes to agent A, the second to B, and so on.

Within this system, especially if more than one teleprospector is involved, *very* careful records on precisely when an appointment is made must be kept. And is, "Yes, but I don't have my book with me. Call tomorrow and we'll set a time," an appointment? Yes? Or, if no, then what is? At issue is not only who gets that appointment—if it *is* an appointment—but because the others are handed out sequentially, who ends up with each of the others will be determined by this.

As always with these appointments, results can be very uneven; the first could be rock solid, the second iffy, the third solid but with less potential than the second, and so on, ad infinitum.

If I sound like a paranoid New Yorker in suggesting that these can become major issues, I deny the paranoia. Problems born of unclear boundaries can make anybody anywhere equally crazy.

ASSIGNED BLOCKS OF CALLING TIME: ANOTHER OPTION

Blocks of time is another possibility. Appointments culled during stint 1 go to agent A, while the next batch goes to B.

However, here, as in most teleprospecting, appointment quality varies widely. Also, in stint 1, there may be no appointments, while stint 2 breaks all previous records on productivity!

"LUCK-OF-THE-DRAW"

"Luck-of-the-Draw" is an oddly interesting alternative; it comes in two variations. You can number the appointments, then ask salespeople to draw corresponding numbers from a hat, *or* the numbers in the hat may define who will have first *choice* on the appointments available.

However, as we all know, some people do awfully well with this kind of thing, while others never so much as find a dime on the sidewalk!

Nor would it work simply to *rotate* the order in which those in the pool could *select*; as sure as sunrise, it would be on the day when there wasn't one good appointment in the bunch that the agent who'd never found a dime would have first choice.

WHAT'S BEST—AND WORST?
SPECIFIC RECOMMENDATIONS

If you're working with a pool, a system that requires appointments to be parceled out *after they've been made* is so open to *feelings* of misuse—valid or not—that probably your safest course is to stay away from it.

Of the other options mentioned, the one I recommend is to assign, in advance, specific blocks of calling time to securing appointments for specific salespeople. This option also strengthens your ability to *get* quality teleprospected appointments. It enables the caller to personalize the conversation in a way simply not possible with, "One of our representatives—."

As temporary emergency backup *only*, assigning individual appointments in a fixed predetermined sequential order offers the advantage of getting more people out into the field faster. If you are one of these people, it may make sense for you, but as with the primary recommendation, the other negatives persist.

CERTAIN NEGATIVES ARE DECEPTIVE; POOLS NEED PATIENCE!

However, some of these negatives are deceptive; now you see them, now you don't. Indeed, there will be days on which the results will be terribly uneven, but *with enough time, all else being equal,* they do balance out. This balance is confirmed by industry historical data, but also by universal laws. Flip a coin 100 times; heads and tails do fall amazingly close to what the mathematically predetermined odds predicted. However, the key is, *you must throw it 100 times.* If your first 10 throws run, for example, 8 to 2, that does not mean the *system* is at fault. In short, you must be patient.

NOT STARTING SOON ENOUGH MAKES PATIENCE DIFFICULT

Frequently, patience is difficult. Quite commonly even excellent salespeople wait far too long before starting, putting themselves under tremendous pressure to come up with appointments immediately; usually the main issue in these cases is a cash flow which by then has become distressingly tight.

You don't have to live like that! Instead, you can plan it out and set it up *far enough in advance*; then go on about your other business as this aspect of your overall prospecting efforts comes to fruition.

CHAPTER 7

How to Hire, Compensate, and Work With Independent Teleprospectors

MAKE PEACE WITH THE EXPENSE

If you decide to use outside teleprospecting help—in whatever form, from whatever source—it's important to make peace in advance with the cost. When you're not at peace, you're set up to push too hard, to not give whatever approach you're using a fair trial, and even to begrudge payment. None of this enhances your productivity.

LOTS OF VARIABLES IN HOW AND HOW MUCH TO PAY

In planning your independent teleprospector budget, you face an extraordinary quantity of variables, with not much frame-of-reference hard data *relative to independents* to help you.

Geography matters; where you live powerfully affects what you must pay for someone good, but even within the same geographical confines, payment structures differ: straight hourly rate, or base rate plus bonus, or—what?

SOURCE MATERIAL CONFUSING

If you think you have hard data on how others are dealing with these issues in *relation to independents*, be careful!

If broad-based hard data on *independents* exists, I have been unable to locate even a trace of it. What data is readily available is virtually always based on regimented operations, sometimes in-house but far more commonly through service firms, and is inadequately labeled in that it makes no distinction between regimented and independent teleprospectors. Instead, it suggests by omission that all teleprospectors are created relatively equal, which has nothing to do with reality.

THE REALITY EQUATION: SHARPER TELEPROSPECTORS EARN MORE MONEY

In reality, anyone sharp enough to handle sophisticated insurance soliciting does not need to accept less money, even if insurance work is not immediately available. Anytime, they can walk into any number of other *kinds* of part-time jobs and earn the same money they would make as an insurance independent; easily three times what even a good monkey-with-a-script is paid.

WHY SCRIPTED CALLERS EARN LESS

As defined earlier, a monkey-with-a-script is a relatively poorly paid cold caller of whom very little is expected. Basically, a "monkey" or *scripted caller* reads a simple script into the phone receiver, perhaps merely screening for interest (someone else will then take over to close either the appointment or actual sale). Sometimes a *bit* more is expected, but the bottom line remains: whatever success a scripted caller may achieve is usually intrinsic to what has been prepared for him or her rather than to any special personal talent or skill.

In its own roundabout way, this point leads to the next, which explains why data on monkey-with-a-script—otherwise known as regimented or, scripted caller—wages in your area is relevant, even though what most independents earn is so much higher.

CORRELATION BETWEEN INDEPENDENT AND REGIMENTED PAY SCALES?

Granted, in a sampling as small as the one taken for this book, it could be coincidence, but when a pattern emerges this often and without exception, it is worth passing along.

There *seems* to be a *rough* correlation of 3 to 1 between what independents and scripted callers are paid. For example, if a scripted caller earns $5 to $8 an hour, in the same state—*ballpark*—the range for a good independent will be $15 to $24. However, although compensation for any particular individual independent may sometimes actually fall below the norm, someone who's really extraordinary not uncommonly earns *substantially* more.

IF LOCAL PAY SCALE INFORMATION IS NOT READILY AVAILABLE

If you don't *have* operations employing scripted callers in your area, look for figures in a comparable area. Service firm information is usually not difficult to obtain; call and ask.

GEOGRAPHICAL GUIDELINES

In summary, answers to the following two questions will provide you with your best outside data frame of reference on what to pay an independent teleprospector in your area:

1. What do other agents pay *local* independents, *for comparable services?*
2. *Keeping in mind a loose correlation of 3 to 1*, what do *local* service firms pay scripted callers?

However, it's still not simple; there are additional variables.

PAY IN SMALL TOWNS IS GENERALLY LESS THAN PAY IN COMPETITIVE BIG CITIES

Even excellent independents in small towns generally earn less than those in large cities, partially because there are not as many competitive insurance operations and partially because other *kinds* of jobs that pay as well are not as plentiful.

NATURE OF LEAD PRODUCT/APPROACH AFFECTS COST OF TELEPROSPECTORS

However, wherever you live, answers to the following two-part question are major considerations in determining an appropriate pay range:

1. What is your door-opener product?
2. How much sophistication will a teleprospector need to present it effectively?

As mentioned earlier, in the Borough of Queens, City of New York, Ed Lennon's door-opener is car insurance. His teleprospectors are high school kids, whom he pays a couple of dollars over minimum wage per hour, which gets him what he needs.

However, "The problem is to keep them calling prospects, instead of their boyfriends," he grumbles, a concern often shared by managers of far larger-scale regimented teleprospecting operations all over the country.

But, also all over the country other, far more sophisticated callers earn substantially more money.

CUTTING CORNERS ON COST PUTS YOU AT DISADVANTAGE

To offer less than the going rate, anywhere, for an independent teleprospector who will be in direct neck-and-neck competition with the *best* other teleprospectors *and licensed agents who do their own calling* in your area doesn't really make sense.

"A lot of people don't understand the value of a good telephone solicitor," comments Rayda Roundy, an extraordinary and extremely well-paid teleprospector in Vista, California, "so they don't pay them enough. It's a big mistake. Every sale coming from an appointment I set up would not have been made without me."

HOW TO PAY: FORM AND STRUCTURE

In regimented teleprospecting operations, life is tidy—or is supposed to be. Each setup has a structure defining what is expected of everyone; how everyone is to be compensated for meeting those expectations has a common clarity transcending geography.

However, independent teleprospector compensation *structures* are widely diverse, often varying even within the same agency. Frequently the arrangement is simply whatever both sides find agreeable. Second-generation Phoenix, Arizona, P&C specialist Bud Davidson has had a lot of experience hiring teleprospectors over the years. His agency has 42 salespeople. "It's difficult," he says. "There is no panacea for payment for this effort. Some want a plain salary, some want a salary plus a bonus per appointment. Some want commissions per sale, and some agencies do pay it, but we don't. Long range, it doesn't work. It gets too expensive."

COMMISSION/BONUS ARRANGEMENTS

Yet many *teleprospectors* do not want a commission arrangement; they believe it's too iffy on whether they would be paid.

Trust is a big issue; in smaller towns, there seems to be more of it than in large cities. Sometimes it's extraordinary—on both sides—while at other times, the lack of it is an excellent reason to not even consider a commission percentage or bonus *per sale*. Teleprospectors fear they will not be paid; agents fear the teleprospector will call potential clients to "check up" on whether money is owed the teleprospectors, which of course does nothing to enhance a potential client's confidence in anyone concerned!

For those who still choose to explore a commission participation arrangement, options include a straight percentage, or a base salary, plus

1. a smaller percentage, sometimes decreasing as the sale and consequent total amount of money to be paid to the teleprospector grow larger, or

2. a set bonus, based on the range the sale falls into; for example, if the agent's commission is between X and Y, the bonus is A, between Y and Z, the bonus is B

PERILS OF PAYING PER APPOINTMENT

As in per *sale* commission/bonus arrangements, mutual good faith is also an issue when agents pay either entirely or partially per *appointment*.

Think about it! If you are paying me per appointment, believe me, I can get you *lots* of appointments! Some will be terrible; for example, if a prospect tells me his brother handles his insurance, I'll point out the advantages of keeping his brother on his toes by getting an absolutely free second opinion. Indeed, you'll get the appointment, but not the sale.

I can hard sell you, too. You'll go way out of your way for people who have no interest in seeing you, but so what? Because I insisted that you were right around the corner, *they* said why not? It got rid of me; they'll get rid of you when you get there.

And yet you'll be reluctant to fire me. Why? Because I'll also get you *lots* of *good* appointments. I *could* get you *only* good appointments—but that's not what you're paying me for!

"GOOD" APPOINTMENTS DEFINED

Carol Kitrosser, a long-time true survivor in Manhattan's highly competitive business insurance market, describes succinctly what constitutes a "good" cold-call appointment: "When you arrive, they're expecting you. They know why you're there. They're ready to talk, to look seriously at what you have to offer."

PER GOOD-APPOINTMENT-ONLY STILL PERILOUS

In Charleston, South Carolina, Tom Masi pays his one teleprospector a base rate plus per appointment bonus, but the bonus applies only when Tom decides the appointment was "good."

"If we get there and find a no-show," he explains, "or someone who wasn't really interested, we don't count it as an appointment."

However, despite the fact that this works for Tom and, here and there, others, paying only for "good" appointments contains such serious potential for abuse by the agent—and for the *perception* of abuse by the teleprospector, which can be just as damaging—as a general rule, you're much better off exploring other options. Indeed, the teleprospector has every right to wonder *was* the appointment "bad," or did the situation change after it was made, or did the agent blow it?

EVEN WITH INTEGRITY, PER APPOINTMENT PAYMENT PROBLEMS LOOM

Even with absolute integrity on both sides, bad appointments—ones that will seriously waste your field time—remain a natural hazard of insurance industry teleprospecting. To learn from these appointments how to cut down on them in the future is constructive, but to assign blame, with the teleprospector's compensation riding on the outcome, is to build additional negative tension into a situation already stressful enough.

Be *very* alert to any outside firm which charges on a per-appointment basis. Once again, even when everyone involved acts with integrity, the raw material for serious future conflict remains intrinsic to the structure.

BUT GETTING WHAT YOU NEED TAKES PRIORITY

However, to lose a good independent teleprospector because you could not agree on a compensation *structure* would be unfortunate. Your first (although never *only*) concern must to be to get what you need, and every alternative discussed here *is* used somewhere, which means it is usable.

KEEP IT SIMPLE!

With one exception, I recommend you keep it as simple as possible by paying a flat hourly rate.

If you're dealing with callers new to insurance, start them at the low end but raise them quickly: the first raise at the end of the first 4 or 5 calling sessions, the next after 8 or 10, and the next after 20. If they're naturally talented, bright, and conscientious and you're doing your part in how you work with them, with each call, their skills should improve. Consequently, very quickly, they should be well worth the higher rate. Thus, their incentive to do their best becomes, quite simply: If they do well, you'll keep them; if they don't, you won't.

THE EXCEPTION

In Syracuse, New York, Charlotte Crandall manages three separate insurance professional associations.

"If a membership is not renewed, we call to find out why," she begins. "In our last fiscal year, we had 114 new members, but lost 100 former members, some to transfers, disability, retirement, or death. Some left the business, but the balance who let their memberships lapse did so because they *simply weren't making enough money.* They had to cut down on expenses wherever they could, especially if they had families to feed."

If this touches a nerve, you're not alone; any situation which affects this many people deserves serious attention.

In this situation, obviously you need to keep your cash outlay as low as possible. Therefore, *under these circumstances*, if you can find someone who will work on a straight commission, or on a slightly smaller commission plus *low* hourly-rate basis, it may end up eventually costing you more, but at least can help keep you in the game until you're in a better position to pick and choose from a wider variety of options.

IF IT'S NOT WORKING—WHEN TO FISH ANYWAY, WHEN TO CUT BAIT

But whomever you hire, with whatever payment structure, if after the first few sessions, you find you're not getting what you need, it's important to sit down with your teleprospector to see whether the two of you can figure out why. Perhaps it's your teleprospector's fault, but perhaps not. Assumptions without investigation can be expensive. Until you get to the root of the problem, you'll not only have the same difficulties with someone else, you'll continue to fire teleprospectors who may actually be excellent, each time losing whatever you've invested in hiring and training them.

If it *is* the teleprospector's fault, perhaps it is easily correctable. As a consultant, I've sat and listened to teleprospectors call, often finding flaws in how they handled their material which, when pointed out, cleared up *immediately*. But sometimes, the problem is your list or your lead product, or, perhaps, you are requiring too much information on a first-contact call. Throughout this book, you will find information to help you in your investigation.

However, if even with excellent support from you, they still cannot meet your reasonable expectations—replace them.

MONITORING CALLS

Whether troubleshooting or merely training, hearing both ends of the conversation is more valuable than is hearing only one. All you need is a second phone, a double jack, and residency in a state where listening in on phone calls without informing everyone on the line is not illegal.

WITH INDEPENDENTS, BIG CHANGES

Most effective days of the week and times of the year are covered elsewhere because they are major factors regardless of who is calling, but how you structure your *teleprospector's* hours will very much affect your results.

When you bring in an outsider, the *nature* of your cold calling changes. It now takes place in far more tightly-defined blocks of time, and you must be sensitive to someone *else's* burnout point rather than your own.

READY, GET SET, R-E-L-A-X!

Anyone with any experience knows that stress and burnout are big issues in cold calling. Coffee, soda, or perhaps fruit juice near the phone can be important for any teleprospector's voice, as well as morale. As often as not, the mechanics of collecting the drink can be as important as the drink itself. It definitely helped me to stop periodically and get ice for a glass from which I usually sipped diet soda, the bottle never too far away.

At times—perhaps every hour or so—I needed to stop for a few minutes and physically stretch, but additional activities could get me out of the calling rhythm, a rhythm I had worked hard to build and wanted to keep.

This is highly individual. Of those who work full seven- or eight-hour days, some do better with long, relaxing lunch hours; others if they hardly break at all. Whether you're dealing with yourself or someone you've hired, this issue needs attention.

FOUR-HOUR CALLING STINTS—YES OR NO?

It is widely believed that a calling stint should consist of no more than four hours; that after four hours, callers burn out.

But you must remember that virtually all of the source data on which these numbers are based originates in regimented group operations, where the work is extremely repetitious.

Among *independents*, who burns out when is highly individual.

Occasionally, an independent works full time, five days a week, but among independents everywhere, this is the exception. More often, they are part time, measured either in number of hours per day or number of days per week.

If you have the option of an independent teleprospector working for you in blocks of either four hours on different days or blocks of full days, go with the full days. On balance, you will come out ahead.

MAINTAINING CONTINUITY IN HOURS

The trouble with four-hour stints is, you lose continuity.

Remember, with a well-paid independent, you are usually trying to reach people at a level not always readily reachable. If I call Mr. Jones at 10 A.M., perhaps he is unavailable, *but I learn that he will be in after 2:00.* Ms. Smith is out, but will be in at 1:00. Mr. Johnson spoke to me—at 11:00—and is interested—but can't really give me his attention until 4:00.

Often I've called the same person three or four times in one day and wound up with a friendly, sympathetic secretary, ready to put me through the moment the prospect is anywhere in sight. However, a week later, probably she wouldn't even remember me.

If the caller leaves after four hours, all these very tenuous connections and all information collected earlier on contacts which might have been made later that same day go down the drain.

MAINTAINING CONTINUITY IN DAYS

If I were calling for two days rather than one, I found it best to make the days sequential. I might learn on Tuesday that the prospect will be in on Wednesday at 9:00, while Thursday's schedule is often not yet available.

SWITCHING DAYS

Occasionally I came across prospects available only on certain days of the week. If they were important enough (for example, if I were calling within a particular profession, and there weren't that many names) after I'd collected enough data—perhaps once a month—I would switch days to facilitate reaching those otherwise unavailable.

HOW TO FIND INEXPENSIVE INDEPENDENT TELEPROSPECTORS

If your door-opener product is as simple as the car insurance review Ed Lennon offers through his high school student callers, by all means contact high school job placement counselors. College kids also are often available for not much money, if the hours fit their class schedules. Organizations for retired or handicapped people can be excellent resources. And according to the long-time president of a New Jersey–based teleprospecting firm, one of his all-time best cold callers was on a prison work release program!

OTHER EXCELLENT SOURCES

Always, when you find someone good, ask who they know. Recommendations are often your best source.

In addition, listen to anyone who cold calls you, on any product. *If you have a screener, tell him or her to let cold callers through.* When you hear someone you like, get contact information, but also ask what they're earning. For unsophisticated work at only somewhat over minimum wage, extraordinary solicitors beyond your budget may nonetheless know others not quite as good, or expensive. Even without an immediate opening, it pays to collect contact information; circumstances change.

THE PRINTED WORD

Flyers in supermarkets, banks, churches, synagogues, adult education institutions, or on any other community bulletin board can be productive. Newspaper ads are also fine, and don't overlook the smaller community papers.

SAMPLE ADS

The following are sample ads you might want to use *if your operation requires relatively little of those you hire.* You can do much more with a flyer; your cost is in the paper and distribution, not number of words. If you use a newspaper, keep your wording tight; here, cost is based on space.

Fill in the blanks on dollar amounts as appropriate to your part of the country.

> *EARN EXTRA $$! Part time, no experience necessary. Like talking to new people? Good on phone? Flexible day/eve hrs. No selling. Call Joe, XXX-XXXX, between (hours).*

Or, be specific when you mention the money:

EARN EXTRA $$! Part-time phone work, no selling, no experience necessary. Start $_____ per hr. Call Joe, XXX-XXXX (time).

HOW TO FIND SHARPER TELEPROSPECTORS

If you need people considerably more sophisticated, most of the sources listed in this section remain valid, except that now you're offering more money and defining your needs accordingly.

The following is a sample newspaper ad:

CALLING TOP COLD-CALLERS! No selling. Insurance agent needs smart part-time telephone help. Flexible hrs. Start $_____ to $_____ , fast raises. Experience setting up appointments preferred, not required. Call Joe, XXX-XXXX (time).

It still pays to take notice of solicitors who call you, but tell your screener to do most of the listening, and to let through only those who are excellent.

A local theater group can also be a good source. Amateur actors run the gambit on economic stability, but most beginning professionals live pretty much hand to mouth waiting for their next acting job. With what you're offering—fast cash and flexible hours—you have an excellent shot at some good people. Actors tend to learn quickly, and to get into the "role" of a solicitor with gusto, *provided the money is attractive.* If you live in an area with lots of professionals, take ads in their industry newspapers. Here, you might run something on the order of

ACTORS NEEDED, TELEPHONE WORK, part time, flexible hours, start $_____ hr, fast payment, no selling. Call Joe, XXX-XXXX (time).

In the same general ballpark as actors, your local radio station might be willing to pass your name on to those who apply for jobs as announcers. If you call and ask, the worst they can do is say no, which is something certainly all of us have learned to live with!

Here, also, schools are a good source, but probably you'll need college rather than high school students. A broadcasting or acting school can be an especially good hunting ground.

DON'T NEGLECT YOUR OWN BACK YARD!

Yet often the best telephone solicitors you could hope for are right in front of you. They are agency customer service reps or, in smaller organizations, a secretary thoroughly familiar with the terminology and good on the phone. This is a common and often successful arrangement. Usually they call for perhaps an hour a day, making burnout much less of an issue. Continuity is also easier. To fit in a few extra calls later following up with those who were not available earlier is rarely a problem.

INITIAL SCREENING

In hiring outsiders, it is important that your initial screening be *over the phone*; be sure to allocate sufficient time when you will be available to receive calls. Also be sure to ask at least a few *open-end* questions, such as "Tell me about yourself," or "What are some of your other interests?" Remember, sometimes they'll need to ad lib.

FIND A VOICE "IN SYNC" WITH YOURS

Be particularly aware of an applicant's voice, not only whether you like it, *but how well does it mesh with yours?*

Years ago, I called for a man with a heavy Middle Eastern accent. Because I was his introduction—his "calling card"—often when he arrived for the appointment, he was too far from what the prospect had expected.

There's no question that this worked against him. Your voice suggests a particular style; this is what prospects are agreeing to meet with. Does your teleprospector match your *style*?

WHAT'S IN A NAME?

An innocuous name, or at least one in sync with yours, is best; again, your teleprospector is your calling card. This does not mean they must *have* a compatible name. The game is, you create it between you; that's the name they'll use when calling for you.

CONTINUE TO COLLECT NAMES AND NUMBERS

If you continue to receive calls from your earlier recruitment efforts after your needs have been met, take the names and phone numbers anyway. Even good teleprospectors are often transient; you may need a replacement on short notice.

YOUR "ASSOCIATE," NOT YOUR "TELEPROSPECTOR"

How would you feel if prospective business associates had others call you because they felt you probably would not be interested in whatever they had to offer, so why waste their time and/or suffer your rejection personally?

Inexpensive callers, like Ed Lennon's high school kids, are obviously cold callers. But at more sophisticated levels, teleprospectors become your "associates" on the phone, in subsequent correspondence, and when you finally meet the prospect. Be sure they understand this!

PAY PROMPTLY!

Remember, teleprospecting is just about always plan B; it's what people do for money while waiting for plan A to materialize. Not paying immediately (preferably cash) is a great way to lose terrific teleprospectors to your competition very quickly!

MALE OR FEMALE TELEPROSPECTORS: WHICH ARE BETTER?

From the Atlantic to the Pacific, the consensus is—women are generally better teleprospectors than men, *especially* in the south, calling "southern gentlemen" prospects.

"The 'southern gentlemen' factor definitely comes through," says Antoinette Hondroulis, an independent in New Orleans, Louisiana.

"A southern gentleman is not going to be rude to a lady," adds Suzanna Edwards, a producer who does her own cold calling in Fort Worth, Texas, "but it's more than that. Women are more sensitive to nuances than men, more likely to recognize and follow intuitive feelings. And we're better listeners."

In Vermont, multi-agency owner Paul Poulos picks up on the same point, but without reference to southern anything. "Women do better," he says. "They're more sensitive, more compassionate."

Although basically I agree, I've known men who were excellent also, superior to many women. And an excellent teleprospector is, of course, what you are seeking.

BOTTOM LINE: GENDER IS SECONDARY!

The bottom line? Gender is secondary. Always talk to anyone you believe might meet your needs; hire whoever you think/feel is best.

CHAPTER 8

Organizing Your Campaign: Ten-point Checklist And Pick a Partner?

ESTABLISHING A START-UP DATE

Before you determine your start-up date—the specific day and hour at which you, your partner (if you have one), or someone you (or you and your partner) have hired will pick up the phone and dial your first cold-call number—you must estimate how much time you will need to make all essential step-by-step planning decisions and to acquire what's necessary to support those decisions.

ADEQUATE FINANCIAL RESOURCES—PLAN A AND PLAN B

You will need money, enough to cover your initial expenses until the operation begins to pay for itself. As you read

125

through the following checklist, you might want to think in terms of plan A and plan B. Plan A would be your first choice. Be careful not to underestimate how much you'll need. As mentioned before, but important enough to repeat: too much pressure to make any project pay for itself too soon has an insidious way of actually delaying the results you seek.

TEN-POINT CAMPAIGN CHECKLIST

Whether your only caller is yourself, only for a few hours each week, or whether your situation is more complicated, to put together a successful teleprospecting campaign, you need all the following elements, presented in no particular order of importance because each is an integral part of the overall process:

1. A time to call
2. A place from which to call
3. Someone to do the calling
4. People to receive the calls—a list of names, preferably *with phone numbers*
5. Something to say to those you call—a presentation also known as a pitch
6. An appointment book or other means to make immediately accessible to the caller information on when you are available
7. A confirmation/rescheduling process
8. Clerical support systems (this subject will be dealt with in greater detail in Chapter 11)
   a. A quick system for recording necessary information on each call
   b. A system for writing up appointments

    c. A system for follow-ups and callbacks

    d. *Initial* other data collection, to help you refine your overall campaign (there's often a tendency to overdo this, which can seriously detract from time spent actually calling)

9. Sales material, if you're planning supplementary mailings

    a. Possibly printed matter

    b. Basic form letter(s), to be personalized as necessary

10. Other materials

    a. Clerical supplies, such as, scratch paper and pens (more on this will be spelled out in Chapter 11)

    b. *Maps*, if whoever is calling—you or someone you've hired—is not familiar with the geographical area being solicited

    c. A watch or clock (If invited to call back at a specific hour, to do so you must keep track of the time.)

Some of the items included have been discussed in previous chapters; some will be explored in greater detail in this chapter; others will be addressed later.

GO IT ALONE, OR PICK A PARTNER?

Among other advantages, a partner can broaden your options in a number of areas covered by the checklist. I've known people who worked strictly two by two, but also some who paired off for particular projects only, possibly working on more than one project at a time, each with a different partner, while also reserving time for strictly solo pursuits.

MALE OR FEMALE?

Male-female partnerships offer numerous advantages. If you visit prospects at home, some will feel more at ease welcoming a man and woman rather than men only. Nor is it only in New York City that in going into the home of a *complete* stranger (remember, these are teleprospected appointments, not referrals), a woman may not only feel safer, but be safer, with a male partner. Despite exceptions, biologically and through socialization processes still very much operative today despite Women's Lib and all that stuff, on balance, I firmly believe that as a group, women are more intuitive than men, while men tend to be more grounded in nuts and bolts action-oriented external world thinking.

Certain people are far more likely to listen to and to take seriously someone of one sex more so than the other.

In summary, a partnership incorporating into itself the *balance* between the sexes can indeed enhance its competitive edge. But obviously sex is only one of many considerations.

DEFINING WHAT YOU SEEK IN A PARTNER

If you work with a partner, do you want their expertise to be similar to yours or to complement it? This, of course, can be decided project by project, partner by partner.

SELECTING A PARTNER WHOSE EXPERTISE IS SIMILAR TO YOURS

Occasionally, the *only* time a prospect will see you really is next Friday at 10 A.M.. If that slot is already filled, but you and your partner have similar expertise, you can split up and handle both. The same fail-safe factor operates if one of you cannot keep an appointment. *Rescheduling is always high risk*; some will be lost.

If your project requires sensitive handling—or, just the opposite, if you've hired the least expensive outside teleprospectors you could find—either you or your partner can remain on site for whatever backup/supervision may be in order, while the other follows through in the field.

PARTNERS WITH COMPLEMENTARY EXPERTISE

Although it's possible to do well with expertise in only one area, with more than one, you substantially broaden your options on teleprospecting approaches/lead products as well as your opportunities for increased total sales to the same client base.

SHARING OLD CLIENTS VERSUS
CROSS-CATEGORY SELLING TO NEW CLIENTS

Cross-category selling is *not* about sharing clients' names; it is not about an L&H or P&C producer, or perhaps a business or personal lines specialist, handing over his or her files to another producer with expertise in another area, who will use the name of the original agent as a referral-based door-opener.

AGENCIES EXPAND PRODUCT RANGE

Nor is it about an agency extending its product range. In Queens, New York, for example, Ed Lennon handles only personal insurance, but is considering expanding to include business. If he does, those among his current clients who also have business needs—*many of whom were obtained through cold calling or subsequent referrals by those obtained through cold calling*—will constitute his start-up business client nucleus, thereby further augmenting the return on his original teleprospecting investment.

WHAT ELSE IT'S NOT ABOUT

Nor is it about cross-category partnership marketing agencies throughout the country which specialize predominantly in either P&C or L&H bringing in one lone soul, often part time, from the other side of the fence, to somewhat pick up on present clients' other needs.

WHAT CROSS-CATEGORY PARTNERSHIP MARKETING *IS* ABOUT!

Instead, here we are exploring a marketing structure in which two salespeople with contrasting yet complementary areas of specialization, such as, personal L&H and personal P&C jointly teleprospect with one lead product, then both sit down at the same initial appointment with a new prospect to review the prospect's needs in both areas.

ADVANTAGES OF PARTNERSHIP CROSS-CATEGORY SELLING

Ed Lennon uses primarily auto insurance—a relatively simple, *but mandatory personal P&C product*—to open doors for often more complicated L&H sales. In his case, one salesperson sells products in both categories. Perhaps this is an option for you, also.

However, for the moment, let's split Ed in half. We now have two salesmen, one specializing in P&C, the other in L&H.

Because he is now two people, each can extend his original expertise in his own area; each now can present a far broader range of door-opener and initial sale products, some of which will lead to more complicated (and more lucrative!) sales down the road, including those through subsequent referrals, most of which the team can handle, where one individual could not possibly keep up with everything necessary to responsibly, competitively service every need.

CHANGES, CHANGES! HOW MUCH CAN ONE PRODUCER KEEP UP WITH?

Clair Thompson, a commercial P&C salesman in Grand Forks, North Dakota, speaks for many others as well as himself in answering why he personally does not sell L&H, even though he clearly has clients who would buy it from him if he did.

"Frankly, I've got all I can do to keep up with being an expert in the field I'm already in; I don't believe I could wear two hats effectively.

"But it surprises me," he continues, "that so many P&C agencies have not developed their life business. We have a couple of life salesmen, part time, but the opportunities for much more are definitely here."

PARTNERSHIP FACTOR IN REDUCING YOUR COST PER APPOINTMENT

Now narrow it down. Whether they do it or not, if an agency can cut across category lines by bringing in a wider range of expertise, thereby substantially enhancing their return on their initial marketing investment, *so can you!*

In other words, to reduce your teleprospecting cost per appointment considerably, write more business—*in whatever category*—for each teleprospecting client acquired. One very viable way to do this is to team up with the right partner, whose areas of specialization are different from your own.

PERSONAL P&C LEAD PRODUCTS USUALLY BETTER THAN PERSONAL L&H

In evaluating the door-opener value of a potential partner's expertise, the following may be helpful: when properly employed, personal L&H teleprospecting can work beautifully. However, in *most cases, in most parts of the country*, the same amount of effort put into *personal P&C* teleprospecting generally garners more appointments, partially because far more teleprospectors call for personal L&H, which makes the competition stiffer, but also, according to Manhattan P&C specialist Carl Gerson, "The resistance to personal L&H products is stronger, because L&H products require spending disposable income." With P&C—both commercial and personal—in most cases whether to buy it is not an issue; instead, the only "choice" is in the selection of a vendor. But this is only one factor.

CROSS-CATEGORY MARKETING—POINT-COUNTERPOINT!

If you are now considering cross-category partnership marketing, in selecting appropriate complementary expertise, the following may help you to focus more precisely on what you want:

1. More people buy personal insurance than business
2. Some who buy personal coverage also buy business
3. *Virtually everyone who buys business insurance also buys personal.*
4. In markets worth pursuing by teleprospecting, most people who buy personal insurance at some point buy *both* P&C and L&H.

IF YOU'D RATHER FLY SOLO

However, if you'd rather work alone, certainly a partner is not mandatory. *Most* producers work alone, many quite successfully.

A TIME TO CALL

The *time* to call is a multifaceted issue. It encompasses seasonal cycles, days of the week, and hours of the day. Also, certain aspects differ in different parts of the country.

NATIONAL CYCLICAL, SEASONAL CONSIDERATIONS

In structuring an ongoing campaign, you'll need to decide whether you want a relatively steady operation or whether there are certain months when you'll want to increase or decrease your investment. Both personal and business L&H insurance needs often go on hold through the Christmas season, while P&C X-dates are P&C X-dates, no matter when they happen to fall.

Throughout the country, most people who buy houses do so in warm weather: many specifically select summer, often so that children can start attending their new school in September. This is a P&C consideration, but also L&H, since many L&H salespeople teleprospect from lists of recent real estate sales, suggesting new owners protect their new investment by increasing their L&H coverage.

If you are categorizing by profession, mid-March through April is a bad time to call accountants, while late June through August may find schoolteachers scattered to the four winds rather than easily accessible at home after work.

These are *national* seasonal concerns; seasonal concerns can also be *regional*.

REGIONAL SEASONAL AND EMPLOYMENT CONSIDERATIONS

In regions where seasonal weather changes are sharp, considerably more cars are bought during the warmer months, making these months particularly active for predominantly personal P&C salespeople, but also for L&H teleprospectors seeking to use car insurance as a door-opener.

If your territory requires a lot of driving and is in a region where snowfalls are generally heavy, are you better off focusing your teleprospecting efforts during warmer months?

Do major cyclical employment factors in your area create large pockets of cyclical highs and lows in both personal and business income, for example, tourist trade or perhaps the manufacture or packaging of seasonal products? Or perhaps less predictable manufacturing contracts determine high employment as opposed to layoffs, which affect the overall economy.

If any of these employment factors influences your area, are you better off concentrating your L&H efforts on prospects affected by them at times when the prospect's income is highest, and your P&C efforts—if your lead is a price advantage—when income is lowest?

BEST AT-WORK CALLING TIMES—DAYS OF THE WEEK

Tuesdays, Wednesdays, and Thursdays are usually best. It is generally believed that on Mondays, prospects at work are far too focused on catching up from last week while getting oriented to this week, to give you much attention, while on Fridays, they're trying to catch up so they can get home, often leaving early. However, I've never experienced Mondays as different from any other days, except Friday afternoons.

MONDAYS AND FRIDAYS

Especially in summer, many key people leave early for the weekend. But others don't. Bottom line? Friday afternoons—particularly during the summer—are my last choice, but in my calling area, you can catch just as fine a fish on a Friday afternoon as on any other day of the week, sometimes no doubt because Friday has such a bad reputation, your competition tends to be sparser.

However, because the total number of appointments you'll net on Fridays will probably be lower, expect your cost per appointment to be higher.

BROADER GEOGRAPHICAL VIEW

In researching this on a broader geographical basis, I found that others experienced calling on Monday *mornings*, Friday *afternoons*, and *sometimes all day Friday* as less rewarding than calling in the middle of the week, although you still need to be wary of hard-and-fast rules. In Portland, Oregon, Bob Beswick, a salesman who specializes in group L&H, does a lot of his own cold calling and says Friday afternoons are *best*.

"People are in a good mood," he explains. "They're slowing down, looking forward to the weekend. On a Friday afternoon, they're much more likely to agree to see just about anybody about just about anything."

BEST AT-WORK CALLING TIMES—HOURS

Standard business hours are usually best, although certain professions march to the beat of their own drummers. In New York City, editors and literary agents generally get in around 10:00 A.M., often staying until 6:00 or 7:00, while, nationally, many dentists arrive by dawn's early light to accommodate patients hoping to make it to the office by 9:00 after the appointment.

If you're considering calling a group targeted by profession, it can be important to ask yourself which professions are especially common in your area, and when are the people in them most likely to be available by phone?

Sometimes individuals in any profession develop their own slightly off-track patterns, for example, perhaps Mr. Jones, for whatever reason, is usually in meetings all day, so he comes in at 8:00 A.M. to keep up with his paperwork.

To accommodate these groups—prospects whose accessible hours are off-center by personal choice, and those who merely operate within an off-center accepted norm for their profession—you may want to adjust your calling schedule occasionally. I generally noted any off-track availability information as it came up in other calling, then acted on it when I'd collected perhaps a dozen or so extra-early A.M. and/or extra-late P.M. names.

But do be patient; wait until you have enough names. Without this, blindly calling before 9 A.M. and after 5 P.M. will usually get you an awful lot of answering devices.

AT-WORK CALLING—LUNCHTIME?

Calling at lunchtime can be surprisingly productive. Indeed, a lot of people are out, but a lot aren't—while their screeners are! Also, if you don't have the decision maker's name, lunchtime is often as good as any other for getting it. Thus, you will not waste precious minutes later fishing when your prospect is available and you could make your connection immediately if you had the name.

CALLING PROSPECTS AT HOME, NEW YORK CITY AREA

Calling prospects at home on Saturdays and Sundays for personal insurance in my area—New York City—brought mixed results. People go out—socially, and to do errands—which means they can be hard to reach. I also garnered more resentment on weekends than on weekday evenings, *which suggests that some of those reached on weekends might be more amenable to talking with you if you reached them during the week.* However, others were quite pleasant. Weeknight calling worked best on Mondays through Thursdays, from 6:00 to 9:00; Fridays were often a waste of time.

CALLING PROSPECTS AT HOME—EARLY MORNING IN TOPEKA, KANSAS

In Topeka, Kansas, Shari Halloran does full-time "cold calling" both in person and on the phone exclusively for New York Life agent John Scott. Her lead product is—no frills, no gimmicks—life insurance. When she pursues prospects at home during the week, frequently she gets on the phone as early as 7:00 A.M.

"Usually, they're getting ready for work," she explains. "They're rushed; they don't have time to deal with me, so they tell me to call back. I ask, 'When?' and they give me a time, usually in the evening. It breaks the ice. Then, when I do call back, I tell them 'As I promised, I'm calling back.' "

Emphasizing the stability of New York Life as a carrier, and the professionalism of the specific agency her producer, John Scott, works through, for every 10 new contacts she makes, she generally nets 2 appointments.

"I set 'em up, John knocks 'em down," she offers lightly. "He goes out in the blizzards, while I'm home with my family!"

EVENING AT-HOME CALLING—TOPEKA, KANSAS; AND SYRACUSE, NEW YORK

Shari's evening calling generally runs from around 6:00 to 9:30, the time period during which most of the people she reached in the mornings have asked her to get back to them. "I never call after 9:30," she adds.

In Syracuse, New York, Massachusetts Mutual agent Mark Rubin generally calls between 5:45 and 6:30 P.M. "At 6:30, the TV national news comes on," he explains. "I figure most people want to watch it." At 7:00, when the news ends, he gets busy again until 8:00. "I never call past 8:00. Eight is TV prime time," he adds. "People have shows they want to watch."

"What about interrupting their dinners?" I asked.

"Well—," he answered, "if they're obviously chewing, I'll ask, 'Am I disturbing you?'"

SATURDAYS AND SUNDAYS

On Saturdays, Mark generally calls between 11:00 A.M. and 2:00 P.M., while Shari sticks with afternoons only. Saturday nights are bad. "Besides," Mark adds, "you don't want to look like a loser. It's Saturday night; everybody else is out, but here you are, poor slob, working!"

Both find Sunday evenings good: Mark, between 6:00 and 8:00, and Shari between 7:00 and 9:30.

CALLING HOUSEWIVES AT HOME, DURING THE DAY

Way back when certain cold-call training material still used by a number of large insurance companies was first developed, wives were called at home in hopes that they would influence their husbands to buy insurance, so that the wife and children would be protected if the husband were no longer in a position to support them.

Certainly a woman with children and other joint marital assets to protect is still likely to want L&H insurance on her husband, but today, *unless she's at home caring for fairly young children until they are old enough for her to return to the outside work world,* during the day, you're far more likely to connect with her at her office rather than in her kitchen.

However, if your goal is daytime teleprospecting to reach this group, generally your best times are after her husband has left and before he gets home. Young children often take naps in the afternoons; if older, call during school hours.

THE RAINY-DAY ADVANTAGE!

But whenever you call at home—weekdays, or nights, or weekends—if your schedule is at all flexible, intensify your efforts on rainy days; people are less likely to be out.

CHAPTER **9**

Ten-point Checklist
Continued:
Places and Prospects

DO-IT-YOURSELF TELEPROSPECTING—
A SPECIAL PLACE FOR IT

If you do your own teleprospecting, you may want to
establish a special place for it. If you have a partner,
perhaps you can use his or her office, or perhaps there's
an empty office. Even a second desk within your own office
can work well.

The point is, you're accustomed to sitting at your
own desk while you work on other projects. After awhile,
thinking about them becomes very much entwined with
the *space* where you usually work on them; your desk itself
becomes a prime component in the general conspiracy to
distract you.

The general conspiracy is everything around you
and—far more often—everything within you that gets

141

between you and the telephone when, as far as you consciously know, you really are committed to spending a particular block of time teleprospecting, yet somehow it's just not happening.

If you do try a new place/space *strictly for cold calling*, after you get used to the initial unfamiliarity of it, you'll probably be pleasantly surprised by how much it not only supports your decision actually to call, but also enhances your concentration and, consequently, your overall success.

A PLACE FOR INDEPENDENTS

I've cold-called from home. I've called on premises from little cubicle offices in large rooms crowded with more of the same and from opulent private offices with thick carpets and Manhattan skyline views. I've called from uninhabited private offices—one in particular I remember had no window and was loaded with empty cardboard cartons and outdated computer equipment which no one seemed willing to dispose of, even though you could write your name in the dust.

I've called from the offices of the salespeople I was working for while they were out, and sometimes my salespeople arranged with others to let me use their offices, when otherwise empty for a few hours or so.

I've called alone and with others in the room.

One of the sharpest salesmen I ever worked for had his desk at a right angle to mine in his private office. He had arranged his schedule to accommodate working with his computer while I called.

Between us, analyzing any call we felt might teach us anything, we eventually refined the small-business pension design pitch into a masterpiece. Beyond his contributions to the pitch, if anyone I called insisted on more information than I had, he was right there to feed it to me or to take over. When he took over, I simply handed him the phone, then picked up the one on his desk and continued calling until mine was free again. Eventually—*when I was able to connect with the right person*—we were running close to a 50 percent appointment rate!

Someone I trained wound up calling from a card table at the end of an office corridor, which was not too swift on the part of her employer. Because she was highly visible, the quantity of qualified appointments she was raking in was also highly visible. Very quickly others within the same agency hired her away from her original producer for more money, promptly whisking her out of sight, into an otherwise deserted private office.

_____

TELEMARKETING ROOMS

I've also trained people who wound up in telemarketing rooms. I've never called from a telemarketing room per se. Once, in the fallout from a political squabble among several salespeople in a large agency, I was told I could not use empty private offices any more. Although I was an independent contractor employed by specific agents, not an agency employee, I was told to move from my otherwise-empty cubicle office into the agency-employee telemarketing room, which I refused to do. Instead, I quit. However, I stayed; my salespeople made arrangements among themselves to always have one of their private offices available to me, which was actually much more comfortable than the cubicle where I'd started—but comfort was not the issue.

If teleprospectors are basically simply reading scripts, far less concentration is required than if they're working with more complex material. Also, this particular operation was loosely supervised; people talked to each other. I don't mean marathon gab sessions, but enough that unquestionably total productivity suffered. It was a work environment I wanted no part of!

PROTECTING YOUR PERSONALLY DEVELOPED SALES MATERIAL

Furthermore—and I know this was a factor in why my agents found other space for me—if you're working with sophisticated material and a top outsider, whom you're paying accordingly, your investment frequently extends beyond your immediate results. If an especially good telephone presentation evolved from working for a number of different agents, it was mine; I was free to use it anywhere. Nor did I ever mind sharing these with other teleprospectors, as other teleprospectors often shared with me.

However, the presentation I refined with the pension salesman who worked so closely beside me was *his* presentation. In an open telemarketing room, it would have become community property!

PEOPLE TO MAKE THE CALLS

In the previous chapter, we dealt with hiring a service firm. In the next, we'll explore in depth hiring of independents as opposed to doing your own calling, which is why we're barely touching on the issue here.

ENOUGH PEOPLE TO RECEIVE CALLS

When I called The Independent Insurance Agents of Wyoming seeking information for this book, their executive director, Jeannine Opsal, was certainly courteous, but two coyotes who overheard the conversation are still doubled up laughing at the hick from New York who didn't even know that the largest city in Wyoming is Cheyenne, with a population of only 50,000.

"Practically all of the insurance in the state is sold through referrals," Jeannine explained. "The agencies are small—basically mom and pop operations."

"Not in THIS remote, rural setting," responded Larry Houser, in Park River, North Dakota. "There are only 1,800 in our trade territory—only 15,000 in the county."

"But how do you find new prospects?" I asked.

"I know everybody—at least, within a 20-mile radius, and 20 miles encompasses the whole county."

However, he referred me to Clair Thompson in Grand Forks. Clair has, indeed, had success with teleprospecting.

There are two points to all this. You need *enough* people, and they need to be close enough together that you can reasonably travel from one appointment to another without spending so much time driving that you have little left for selling.

And, occasionally, you'll hit a particular target area which is like a small town in that there are already agents there whom everybody knows, likes, and does business with. This came up several times when Manhattan agents I worked for decided to concentrate on smaller, sometimes relatively self-contained communities in upstate New York, in New Jersey, or on Long Island. Sometimes it worked, but sometimes I realized after about a dozen calls that to pursue it any further would probably not be cost effective.

PEOPLE TO RECEIVE CALLS—DON'T UNDERVALUE PHONE DIRECTORIES!

In Charleston, South Carolina, Thomas Masi, sales manager for the Shirley Merrill Agency which specializes in group health and employee benefits, has done a great deal of teleprospecting. Unable to continue because he no longer has time, he now supervises one outsider.

"We use only the Yellow Pages," Tom says. "It works very well. If a business isn't big enough to be listed there, probably it isn't big enough for us to do business with."

But Telephone Marketing Promotions, Inc. president Karen Placek, speaking from Florida, strongly recommends using *only* the A to Z Business White Pages. "Using only the A to Z Business White Pages," she explains, "avoids wasting time with duplicate calls. In the Yellow Pages, businesses are listed by category. Many businesses can be classified under more than one category. The A to Z Business White Pages are strictly alphabetical, thereby eliminating this problem."

KINDS OF BUSINESS TELEPHONE DIRECTORIES

Karen mentions Business White Pages—a strictly alphabetical listing of businesses. In 1991, the New York Telephone Company started a business *section* in its White Pages, in effect, a listing comparable to Karen's Business White Pages. Yellow Pages, of course, are everywhere.

Many large cities offer two Yellow Pages directories: Business to Consumer and Business to Business. A few categories are "Dual"; identical information appears in both books, but sometimes names under the same headings will vary between a business- and a consumer-oriented directory. And sometimes a complete heading will appear in one but not the other. For instance, dentists are listed only in the Business-to-Consumer Directory, while

Nuclear Energy Consultants—imagine the errors and omissions premiums!—are strictly Business to Business.

CITYWIDE RESIDENTIAL AND COMMUNITY DIRECTORIES

If you live in an even moderately large city and do *residential* teleprospecting, a glance at the residential White Pages could seem overwhelming, but the good news is, many cities—New York among them—break down these larger books into individual community directories; for example, in Manhattan, there are separate directories for Greenwich Village, Upper West Side, Murray Hill, and so on. Each of these also includes a Yellow Pages section, listing businesses only in that community.

FIND OUT WHAT'S AVAILABLE

Before you decide which to use, in whatever category, it makes sense to check out the full range of what's available in your particular area. To do this, simply call your telephone business office. Usually there is no charge for any of these directories.

BUT, BEWARE OUTDATED INFORMATION!

However, remember, *telephone directories are updated only once a year*. Your best calling period is shortly after a new edition comes out. Shortly *before*, the old edition can be expensive in that it will waste a great deal of your time with outdated information. In planning your campaign,

you may want to call your local phone company and ask
when the new books will be out.

PRIMARY OBJECTION TO COMMERCIALLY PREPARED LISTS

The primary objection to commercially prepared lists is
that those who compile them sell the same list to as many
customers as possible.

However, so what? If Joe Jones is a valid prospect,
there's no way you can keep others from calling him. But
if he's *not* valid, the right list can save you the *full* cost of
a call, which includes your phone company bill, your time,
and any attendant clerical expenses.

THREE MOST IMPORTANT CONSIDERATIONS IN BUYING PREPARED LISTS

As the three most important considerations when buying
real estate are location, location, and location, with any
list, the three most important factors to consider are up to
date, up to date, and up to date.

The biggest call response time wasters are

1. "That number has been disconnected."

2. "Mr. Jones is no longer with the company. What is
    this in reference to?"

3. If your list is geographic, "That number has been
    changed. Please hold for the new number," is just
    as bad, because if the company has moved, fre-
    quently it is no longer in the area in which you are
    seeking appointments.

BUSINESS BREAKDOWNS AVAILABLE
THROUGH COMMERCIAL LISTS

Even though the geographical *business* breakdowns by neighborhood in many community directories are excellent (if up to date!), if the breakdowns are still so large you feel overwhelmed, a *good* commercial list can bail you out. Also, community directories classify by *kinds* of businesses, which may or may not be relevant to your needs. If not, it's a waste of time to find yourself in the same office building on four separate occasions because the appointments were scheduled through product or service category, when a commercially prepared list based on location could have allowed you to schedule all four on the same day.

Commercially prepared lists can also give you other selective information not available in phone directories. Perhaps your approach/lead product requires you to know number of employees and/or nature of the products and/or services offered, and/or—think it through. Write it down. What do you want?

The right list will also help you to avoid wasting time calling what appear in the phone book to be local companies but are actually branches of far larger organizations, often with benefits handled out of state.

REACHING THE RIGHT PERSON

Commercially prepared lists can give you the name of the proper person to ask for when you call. "Can you tell me who handles—" is a wide-open invitation to, "What is this about?" which, at best, wastes time. At worst, it can kill it for you on getting past a screener who would have let you through had you simply asked for a specific person.

_____

PRESIDENT/OWNER OR CONTROLLER?

You want decision makers. Sometimes these are the owners/presidents, but often the owners achieved that position because of their *marketing* skills, not their understanding of money. Often the *real* decision makers as far as your needs are concerned, whose advice will virtually always be accepted, are the controllers, financial vice presidents, or accountants.

When the president/owner refers you to a subordinate, certainly this can be a door-opener, in that the subordinate probably will take you more seriously more quickly.

But owners are often more difficult to reach than money people. In pursuing contact with owners, you'll be pursuing contact with people who really are on the phone, out, or in meetings most of the time, and you'll face tougher screeners. You'll also face appointment calendars which often are far more crowded than those of the money people. Unless reviewing insurance has a reasonably high priority at the particular time you happen to call, you may be sloughed off by an owner, while a controller will at least meet with you, thus beginning the relationship from which a sale could indeed eventually materialize.

There's also a political consideration. Remember the pension design salesmen described in Chapter 2, who so often had presented their proposals to the top people only to be shot down by the money people? If you come in through the money people, you begin with their support, which can be critical later.

If you've requested the controller's name but the company is not large enough to have a controller, most likely you'll be referred to the owner, which is fine. In these cases, the owner probably is your best contact.

In summary, the question you'll have to decide for yourself—because there are valid arguments both ways—

is: when you define your preferred contact person for a commercially prepared list, is it the owner or the money person?

COMMERCIAL LISTS OFFERING SPECIFIC RESIDENTIAL INFORMATION

In *residential* teleprospecting, the proper list can tell you who has recently gotten married or had a baby or bought a new house or—you name it. If you have a specific lead product, whose needs is it most likely to meet?

SELECTING COMMERCIALLY PREPARED LISTS

Open your Yellow Pages to Mailing Lists. If your area has both Business-to-Business and Business-to-Consumer directories, you'll find it in Business-to-Business.

Call *at least three* of those listed, and

1. Listen carefully to *their* telephone presentations.

2. Ask how long they've been in business.

3. Ask permission to contact some of their customers.

4. Ask what breakdowns they can give you within the list; number of employees, or if personal, age, and so on, and what do they charge for these breakdowns?

5. Compare prices. Be careful of "cheap." Usually, cheap means out of date.

6. Ask how recently whatever they want to sell you has been updated.

Here, you want guarantees. If X percent are out of date, how much of a refund or credit will they give you? But you still need to be careful; a refund will not cover your losses on time wasted calling bad (out-of-date) numbers.

7. *Be sure the list includes phone numbers.*

In New York City, at last count, to call Information cost 50 cents. Or you can hire someone to look up numbers, but even at the cheapest clerical rates out there, this is expensive. And some of the numbers they find will be wrong; remember, phone books are updated only once a year.

8. What is the *physical form* of the list?
    a. Individual file cards?
    b. Stick-on labels?
    c. Printed (possibly by computer) list?
    d. Computer disk?

Computer disks are great—if you have the equipment and a teleprospector who knows how to use the disks. There's no need to recopy any source material, and if you need more space than you initially anticipated in which to make notes, it's readily available to you.

But with most *small* operations, this is rarely the case. Nor does it make sense to deprive yourself of a good teleprospector simply because he or she doesn't know your particular software.

Although I use Word Perfect to write, I've never used a computer while teleprospecting; no one I ever worked for offered me that option. In terms of accurate, up-to-date information, the best—and most expensive— lists *I've* ever worked with consisted of *individual file cards.* Unfortunately, they were so crowded with information, there was little room on them to write the results of the call, which meant the cards needed to be attached—stapled or taped to larger cards which had room for notes—or virtually the whole card had to be hand copied for every appointment or follow-up, which wasted way too much time. Also, staples come out, and tape comes off.

If you're not computerized, by far, my first choice is stick-on labels. For a callback or appointments, a label can be transferred to a file card in only a few seconds.

Printed lists require the most clerical time. Far too often, far too much information for follow-up calls must be hand copied.

9. Don't immediately load up with one supplier; take time to be sure they're giving you what you need.

10. Keep Old Faithful—the phone book—handy.

If, no matter how careful you've been, you still end up with a "bum list," the phone book gives you a fail-safe way of not completely wasting whatever time you've set aside both to call and to keep appointments anticipated from the calling investment.

"BUM LISTS"

A list can be "bum" for a number of reasons. Number one is, of course, it's out of date. But sometimes you'll stake out a particular area only to discover that it is, in effect, a "small town" within your larger calling area, already *very* heavily solicited *and serviced*, perhaps by another agency of the same carrier you represent. Or perhaps your lead product is sophisticated, and nobody's getting it, while in the more educated area you called last week, you were encouraged by very positive responses.

OTHER SOURCES OF LISTS

Again, open your Yellow Pages. Look up Associations, Organizations, and Clubs. All have members. Which lists can you get? Usually chambers of commerce are open with their members' names. Get the number from your phone book, call, and ask.

Mortgage lists can lead you to people who have just bought homes; so can water turn on lists, often sold by Water Departments. Call—or go to—your local City Hall, and do some exploring on any lists at all they might have which would be available to the general public in your area, and helpful to you.

Take a moment to review your own life. Does the college you attended offer names of alumni in your area? Do you have a political club affiliation? Social or health club? What else?

CHECKING OUT DIRECTORIES IN LIBRARIES

Another excellent place to locate names of potential prospects is the library. If your local library is too small, call others within a reasonable travel radius; then go to the nearest town(s) where you can connect with a varied assortment of hardbound directories, some specifically compiled to meet the needs of cold callers. You may then decide whether you want to order one (or more). If you're not quite sure where to begin, make friends with the librarian. Librarians can be an invaluable resource.

Occasionally, you'll find books of names in libraries that you can photocopy, but be aware of the fact that in some cases this is illegal. You need to check. If it is illegal, usually there is a statement to this effect in the front of the book.

FASTER, MORE CONCENTRATED RESULTS
WITH LISTS OF 100 OR MORE

Even if your list is relatively short—perhaps no more than
a hundred names—often you can enhance your results by

1. Skimming
2. Starting in the middle

"SKIMMING" DEFINED

"Skimming" consists of going over a list and eliminating
anyone who, for whatever reason, seems less likely than
the others to become a viable prospect. There's no need to
cross out these names in indelible ink, but if you are
seeking as many qualified appointments as possible *as
soon as possible*, skimming is a viable option.

For example, if I were calling from a business list
which included number of employees, with a lead product
valid for only groups of from 25 to 100 workers, I might
cross out any business with fewer than 30 or more than
95. Companies change size. In this crossed-out group
would be found the largest percentage of those businesses
which had fallen outside the necessary parameters and,
consequently, would be a waste of time.

Also, frankly, if my lead were tax savings, I would
skim out high-cash-with-few-records businesses, such as
real estate rental or restaurants.

RETURNING TO NAMES ELIMINATED EARLIER
BRINGS LOW RETURN

Of course, you can always come back to those you skipped
initially, but with the understanding that you are now

dealing with least likely to succeed numbers. Consequently, your appointment return per hour invested will be substantially lower.

JUMP IN, IN THE MIDDLE; SWIM TO THE BACK!

A number of years ago, a number of hard-data studies showed that telephone solicitors, in any field, usually started at the beginning of the alphabet, with very few actually making it to the end. Therefore, Mr. Aaron got lots of calls, while Mr. Zzxud received very few.

So, they all said, *let's start at the end of the alphabet!*

And that's what more and more are doing today, although it seems that the A's are still way ahead of the Z's. However, *enough* are now starting with Z that the next best step is to start at *approximately* the middle of the alphabet and then work toward the *back*. In my experience, it's *much* better than A, but now also beats Z!

I have no other data on it—because I found no one else who was doing it, which speaks for itself very nicely as to just how uncrowded it actually is in the middle!

Of course, if your list is smaller and more elite, and it's probable that you'll finish it, where you start is irrelevant.

GLEANING NAMES FROM NEWSPAPERS

Although I've never worked for anyone who relied on combing through newspapers for leads, lots of people still do it and find it worth the investment. *Everyone* I discussed it with who does it—combs newspapers for marriages, birth announcements, job promotions, or whatever—uses a preapproach letter.

In whether or not to use newspapers, the size of the area you solicit is a factor. In New York City—and other big, tough, extremely competitive markets, compared to other ways of getting names in most of the same categories—sifting through newspapers not only takes a lot of time, but because so many salespeople with so many other products do the same thing, after awhile *any* call from a salesperson in relation to "the event," whatever it was, can easily be viewed as more of an annoyance than an opportunity.

CHECKLIST CONTINUED IN SUBSEQUENT CHAPTERS—AND USE THE INDEX!

All items on the checklist not covered thus far will be explored in subsequent chapters. Also, for reasons discussed in Chapter 1 (the interconnectedness of all aspects of the overall process) items already discussed will reappear.

Therefore, this reminder is offered: in referring back to the checklist after you've finished the book once, for a complete review of whatever subject especially interests you, be sure to use the index.

CHAPTER 10

Auxiliary Support:
Mailings

AUXILIARY SUPPORT

Auxiliary support is every bit as important as any other
dimension of the overall teleprospecting process. As discussed in the saga of the pension designers seeking contacts with accountants (Chapter 2), even one additional
appointment within a set calling time frame can double,
triple, quadruple, or boost even higher your overall return
on investment.

Some of what you can do to land more appointments (without increasing calling time) *sometimes* costs
more money, but *most* is free, consisting merely of doing
whatever you're already doing more efficiently.

Although one person's answers on how to improve
support effectiveness are not necessarily universally applicable, many of the questions cover common ground.

EXPLORING THE QUESTIONS IN TODAY'S MORE COMPETITIVE MARKETPLACE

The questions need to be explored. Even a decade ago, the competition from other cold callers, offering any number of other products, bore no resemblance to what's out there today. Nor were banks at all in the insurance telephone-soliciting picture as they are in the 1990s. To allow prospects to slip through your fingers through inadequate, outdated backup support is to undermine very seriously your overall chances for success in this business.

A major backup resource is "cold call mailings."

"COLD-CALL MAILINGS"

"Cold-call mailings" consist of *sales material sent to people you do not know who have not been referred to you.* Postsale follow-up, although no longer in the "cold" category, is an extension of it in that any additional business growing from an initial cold call further enhances return on your original teleprospecting investment.

MATERIAL TO SUPPORT SELLING DIRECTLY BY MAIL OR PHONE

Included in this category is material designed to sell directly by mail and/or directly through follow-up phone calls. As discussed earlier, these direct sales operations are usually on a scale far beyond the reach of most individual agents: they are underwritten by organizations *employing* agents.

TELEPROSPECTING-RELATED MAILINGS

The following covers only those areas in which individual insurance agents make individual choices to suit their appointment-related selling styles. Here, as in all other tele*prospecting* operations, your goal is an *appointment*, through which, hopefully, an eventual face-to-face sale will materialize:

1. *Reply requested*, large-scale, one-shot bulk letters, usually thousands, sometimes offering a premium

2. *Newsletters*, usually hundreds, in most cases more than one issue sent to each recipient, laying groundwork for telephone follow-up within a relatively open time frame

3. *Smaller-scale bulk, with fast telephone follow-up*, one-shot, usually in batches of a hundred, specifically stating that you will call soon

4. *Small-scale sharply targeted personalized, with fast telephone follow-up* (can be as few as one or two at a time)

5. *Post initial contact, pre-appointment*, highly personalized, possibly confirming arrangements for additional contact, by phone or in person, and/or possibly including literature

6. *Post sale*, laying the groundwork for add-on business with the same client and referrals to others

REPLY-REQUESTED LARGE-SCALE BULK LETTERS

Often primary carriers bear most of the expense on *large*-scale ZIP Code bulk mailings.

A friend of mine in New Jersey who knew I was working on this book recently sent me a bulk mailing letter from a local insurance agent. I called the agent, who told me he pays approximately $70 per month toward the cost of between 1,000 and 2,000 form letters, which his company mails to addresses within selected ZIP Codes.

I'm not being more specific because my purpose is not to criticize the company. Rather, it is to enhance the effectiveness of a bulk-mailing soliciting process still widely used, which is not nearly as productive as it could be.

The letter was printed on a giant insurance company's letterhead, with the names—addressee and agent—typed in (not even in the same type face as the rest of the copy; the economy with which it had been prepared was immediately obvious), asking readers to send to the agent, in the postage-free envelope provided, their birth date, phone number, and a convenient contact time.

In return, the reader was offered—guess what!—information on life insurance. Although most of the people in this particular ZIP Code were, like the agent, young and single, or unlike the agent, quite elderly, it stressed the value of life insurance in protecting families.

His return, the agent told me, ran between 2½ to 3½ percent. About half, he learned through calling each month, were ineligible, because of age or health problems.

PERSONALIZING LARGE-SCALE BULK L&H REPLY-REQUESTED MAILINGS

Obviously, *very* few bona fide prospects were responding. In talking further with him, a number of selling points specific to his particular situation emerged. None detracted from the necessarily generic tenor of a mailing of this size.

He had selected the ZIP Code where my friend lived because the agent also lived there. The agent liked the neighborhood and also felt it would be especially convenient for evening visits.

Why not say so?

Why not say, for example,

Dear _____,

Please allow me to introduce myself. I am one of your neighbors. I live on _____ Street; we've probably seen each other in *(name of largest local supermarket)*, or perhaps *(name of second largest supermarket or maybe a large drugstore)*.

I'm contacting you because I make my living making sure people like you are protected from being wiped out financially by the kind of personal disasters most of us don't even want to think about. I sell insurance—life and health. Even if you're already covered, as we grow older, our needs change; policies should be periodically reviewed. I'd be happy to stop by at your convenience and do this for you, at no charge.

In the enclosed postage-free envelope, please send me your date of birth, your phone number, and the time you'd prefer to have me call you, or you can call me at _____ anytime.

Thank you.

Sincerely,

He might also point out that his company is historically one of the most financially stable in the world, especially relevent now that the issue of instability has come up with so many others.

Although I'm not suggesting that this is the *only* approach, I am suggesting that you use an approach with color, flavor. What my friend received wasn't even vanilla!

FREE SOLAR CALCULATORS, PENS 'N STUFF

Or perhaps you're offering a premium. Basically, your letter would be the same, except for the "reward" for those who see you.

The negative with gifts is, of course, you'll waste time with people who want only the freebie, although the other side of the same coin is that perhaps you'll also net some valid prospects who, without the gift, would not respond.

BULK-MAILING "FLYERS"

Also in the "bulk" category are reply-requested mailings somewhat on the order of supermarket flyers, usually suggesting superb price advantages, often targeted to specific groups such as property owners or small businesses. The most recent of these I received was P&C, *all* about price. The word "service" was not mentioned.

THE "PERSONAL TOUCH"

And service matters! "Sell them on price, you'll lose them on price," says Paul Poulos, with one agency in New

Hampshire and two in Vermont. This is not intended to suggest that price is not a valid mail-solicitation attention-getter, but in addition to price, *what makes you special?* Stop and think. Is where you live an asset? How long have you been in the business? Because the industry turnover rate is so high, having been around awhile can suggest to potential clients an attractive stability. Or perhaps your family background can help you.

SAMPLE PERSONALIZED P&C BULK LETTER

For example,

Dear _____,

For 25 years, my father (uncle, brother) struggled with the concerns of running a small business very much like yours (or owning real estate very much like yours, or whatever). Consequently, I grew up with firsthand exposure to many of the particular stresses you live with every day in relation to your work.

This is why I believe I can offer you the kind of individually tailored very specialized insurance service you need, at a price probably superior to what you're now paying.

At no charge, I'd be delighted to review the coverage you already have, to see if there's any way I can make it easier and less expensive for you. As I'm sure you already know, needs change; keeping up with them is an ongoing process.

Please send me the following information in the postage-free envelope provided with this let-

ter, so that we can arrange a convenient time to
meet.

_____

_____

_____

Thank you.

Sincerely,

_____

MORE PERSONAL, LESS FORMAL APPROACH IS "IN"

Don't ever be afraid to use your *personal* selling points;
especially, don't be afraid to sound like a human being.
And don't hesitate to lean more toward an informal rather
than formal style, in all your correspondence. It's "in," like
denim and sneakers in offices (unheard of even a generation ago!) and computer bulletin boards through which
complete strangers reach out to others, with a new, genuine friendliness.

_____

BETTER MOUSETRAP? RESPONDING BY MAIL TO BULK-MAILING REPLIES

Walt Worsham, Augusta, Georgia, introduced in Chapter
3 in relation to his *news*letter has developed a system for
processing bulk letter reply cards which may be unique.
With it, his results are quantifiably substantially more
effective, he asserts.

Periodically he sends out batches of 3,000 ZIP Code
reply card bulk mailings, offering assorted premiums. But
when the reply cards come back, instead of calling at that

point, he responds with a personal letter *in which he returns the reply card.*

In the personal letters, he introduces himself, thanks the respondents for their interest, and promises to call soon.

"The stationery and the letter content give all of it an extra measure of respectability. Including their reply cards catches their attention, reminds them that they expressed interest. It also gives them time to think; time they don't have if I call immediately. When I finally do call, they remember. They're expecting me, and are generally much more responsive.

"I think it's especially effective with those who responded because they really only wanted the gift. In the letter, I switch the focus from the gift back to the insurance; get them thinking that maybe they really should look at the insurance.

"Without the follow-up letter, I'll hit a reply card appointment rate of 40 to 50 percent; with it, the range is 70 to 80.

"My company wasn't too keen on it, at first," he adds, "but they can't argue with the results."

NEWSLETTERS

In addition to personalized letters in response to bulk-mailing reply cards, as mentioned in Chapter 3, Walt Worsham also sends a newsletter.

"For some, the content isn't even relevant to their particular business," he readily admits, "but I send it anyway—usually for at least three or four months before I call. People get used to seeing it. It has my picture, so they know what I look like. It gives me identity, credibility. Sometimes they're people I've already met; sometimes they're people I'd *like* to meet; perhaps names I've gotten from a newspaper. But through whatever source I make the initial contact, I'd still never call anyone I hadn't approached first in some way by mail."

In Tacoma, Washington, the Tom Taylors—junior and senior—also send two separate newsletters, but quarterly rather than monthly, to two separate prospect categories: one P&C, the other L&H. Although their lists are generated through personal contacts only, the newsletters—with good, clear, side-by-side headshots of both father and son—keep those contacts active, enhancing the Taylors' competitive edge for follow-up calling, especially as P&C X-dates draw near.

If you decide to invest in a newsletter (there are professional services which will provide the copy for you), *be sure to include your picture*, and don't be shy about the size of it. Visually striking logos and catchy slogans also enhance effectiveness. Remember, what you are really doing with all this is prospecting; your goal is to take the chill out of the "cold" call when, eventually, you teleprospect from your mailing list.

SMALL-SCALE BULK LETTERS, WITH FAST TELEPHONE FOLLOW-UP

In Boody, Illinois, Harry Woolen sends preapproach letters in batches of 100, introducing himself and emphasizing a probable price advantage, following up by phone three days later. Because each letter requires a call, the quantity mailed must be kept manageable. As with all bulk mailings, Harry's results are generally erratic, although on balance productive enough that he continues.

Frequently these smaller-scale mailings emphasize a particular product, placing them very much in the same ballpark with straight cold calling. Both often lead with a catch: a hook.

ALL-TIME MOST SUCCESSFUL GROUP L&H
LETTER, IN LANSING, MICHIGAN

Yet in Lansing, Michigan, agent Craig Beachnaw, offers the following as his all-time most successful group insurance preapproach letter used to penetrate the business insurance market:

> Dear _____,
>
> Are you currently happy with your group medical insurance and premium? I will call you within the next few days to further discuss.

SMALL-SCALE PREAPPROACH BULK MAILINGS
IN NEW YORK CITY

In my experience over the years, in New York, "cold-call" bulk mailings preceding telesprospecting calls rarely made any difference. Most of the salespeople I called for did not send anything first. Remember, you want to maximize your overall return on investment; keep in mind what the cost would have been, for thousands of calls—and all this was before first class postage hit even 29 cents!

SHARPLY TARGETED INDIVIDUAL
PREAPPROACH LETTERS

Individualized letters are the most expensive. Even though you'll eventually develop a basic form, each is still separately prepared. Individually targeted preapproach letters are generally sent to people you know much more about, people who have given you specific reasons to believe they are actually prospects, not merely suspects.

"I'm not sure preapproach letters (in this category) make much difference to the people who receive them," says Mark Rubin, in Syracuse, New York, "but they help *me*. I feel better about making the call."

However, in Portland, Oregon, Bob Beswick, who specializes in business L&H, always starts with a personal letter. "Portland is like a big small town," he explains. "The business community is close knit. Most of the people in it have already heard of me; probably the letter will be read.

"I focus on what I offer that's special. A lot of group L&H plans around here were put in by P&C, not L&H, experts. I emphasize that because of my L&H expertise, probably I can do a better job.

"My clients usually stay with me. Some have been with me for as long as I've been in the business, about 10 years. This speaks for itself on service quality. It's another selling point.

"Starting with a letter, then following up by phone, I usually hit 3 appointments in every 10 calls; 1 becomes a sale."

"A preapproach letter is definitely worth it," says John Linley, director of marketing and sales for the MDS Insurance Group in Rockford, Illinois.

PREAPPROACH LETTERS PEGGED ON AN EVENT IN PROSPECT'S LIFE

Ned Burns, a personal L&H agent at the same agency, agrees.

"Usually, I peg it on an event in the prospect's life," says Ned. "I'll start out, 'Congratulations on your promotion' or 'on buying your new home.'

"'I'd like to meet with you and discuss how these changes are affecting your everyday life. I have some ideas I think might interest you,'" he continues, outlining the letter content. "In a few days, I'll call and introduce my-self."

The stationery tells the recipient that Ned is an L&H insurance salesman. Aside from this, in the initial letter, Ned says very little about himself.

An old and profound sales adage advises, "Never say 'ba ba' when 'ba' will do." However, when the subject is sales support letters, you may need to ask whether "ba" *will* do—at least do as much as you'd like it to. Ned's been in the business nine years and lives as well as works in the Rockford area. Another sentence or so including this information couldn't hurt, although it is also important to keep preapproach letters *short*, and *to the point*.

But keep in mind, no matter how well written, most preapproach letters are still more steak than sizzle, and insurance sizzle is especially difficult to package in writing.

PREAPPROACH LETTERS OCCASIONALLY BACKFIRE

Occasionally, preapproach letters backfire. Occasionally, the prospect or, more commonly the prospect's screener, will turn them around into, "Mr. Smith has your letter. The fact that he hasn't called you means he's not interested," or "I've read your letter; there's nothing to pursue."

POSTINITIAL CONTACT MAILINGS

*Post*initial contact mailings constitute an entirely different category; cost, not whether they'll backfire, is your primary concern. Individual letters following initial contact but prior to your first meeting with a new prospect are collectively expensive. Even working from basic forms, someone still needs to tailor those forms to suit specific situations and actually to write the letter. Also, the supplies—stationery, stamps, and wear and tear on some kind of machine—cost money.

THREE CATEGORIES OF PREAPPOINTMENT MAILINGS

Basically, there are three categories of teleprospecting-related preappointment mailings:

1. "Cold-call" general soliciting
2. Post-initial-call mail support to help obtain specific appointments
3. Confirmation, once an appointment has been set

General soliciting has already been covered; it precedes the first phone call.

Specific mail support *after* that first call but before the appointment has been secured is a different ball game. Basically, there are two major criteria for determining when this kind of follow-up is warranted:

1. The size of the potential sale
2. The amount of time that will probably elapse before the next contact

The first point has a built-in assumption—that there really is a potential sale. Too often when prospects mean "no" instead of saying so, in the name of well-intentioned courtesy or whatever, they respond, "maybe, but not now," or perhaps, "send me some literature; I'll get back to you if I'm interested," which quite commonly is merely an unfortunate waste of time all around.

Nor is it always easy to gauge just how big a particular sale might be, especially if you're using a small-scale door-opener in hopes of larger rewards later.

If you do your own calling, you'll have more flexibility to follow your own instincts in each situation; or sometimes whether you follow up by mail may even be determined by what kind of otherwise uncommitted time you happen to have on any given day.

However, if you hire an outsider, you'll need to be a lot clearer, because you'll need to leave clear instructions.

POSTINITIAL CALL, BUT NO APPOINTMENT YET SAMPLE LETTER

On potentially large sales, when I was told to call back in a month or so, if the conversation had been good—if the prospect had indicated genuine interest and openness—I generally sent something on the order of the following:

Dear _____,

Thank you for your (*1*) time on the phone this morning with my (*2*) associate, Ms. Davis. As (*3*) agreed, we will definitely call you again next month (in two months—whatever). In addition to the specific material you and she discussed, I have some (*4a*) ideas I very much look forward to (*4b*) sharing with you.

Sincerely,

(*5*) Your Name

There's a great deal more to this letter than is probably readily apparent.

1. *Immediately*, it refers to the phone call; this is a memory-jogger, attention-getter.

It takes the letter itself out of the "unsolicited" category. It may also make the deciding difference on whether a secretary will pass it on or dispose of it as junk mail.

2. If you used an outside teleprospector, it transfers the contact from your "associate" to you.

Teleprospectors come and go; you don't want your contacts to go with them! This introduces you, puts your name in front of the prospect. It also suggests that the prospect is special enough to warrant an approach by your "associate," which is much more personal than a call from a telephone solicitor.

3. "As agreed, we will definitely call you..." keeps control.

This is critical. Even a prospect who is genuinely interested can forget. As long as *you* are doing the follow-up *by agreement* you're still in the running, without looking pushy. I *always* asked, "May we call you again?" If I got an "absolutely no," I recognized it as a brushoff and treated it accordingly. I might have *called* again later (people forget and circumstances change), but I would not recommend investing in a letter.

A "yes," *if the potential sale was large enough*, and the prospect seemed genuinely interested warranted the follow-up mailing.

4a. and 4b. "Ideas" and "sharing" are buzzwords.

"Ideas" intrigues, implies creative thought. "Share" is friendly, suggesting a joint problem-solving approach rather than a hard-sell prepackaged I'm-the-expert presentation.

5. In signing your own name rather than the name of your teleprospector, you take final, full control of the contact.

SEND LITERATURE?

Here, there are enormous geographical differences. In some sections of the country where the tenor of life is basically more gentle than in faster-paced large cities, it's common practice to send literature pretty much whenever requested to do so.

In *my* experience, *in New York City*, almost always, a request for literature rated an argument as to why an appointment would be more to the prospect's advantage. Less than this could lose a sale to the competition, while in other parts of the country I realize it could have just the opposite effect. It could offend.

Therefore, where do you live?

If you *do* send literature, it's important to, at minimum, send a note *on your office stationery*, stating that this is the material the prospects *requested* and that you look forward to discussing it further with them when they've had a chance to look at it. You also might want to consider a stamp for the outside of the envelope which reads, quite simply, "Requested Material."

Formal letters can also be effective. Do *not* send generic, blank stick-on notes. If you must use stick-ons, have your name printed on them and, if your operation has a logo, include your logo. Remember, you are selling *your services* much more than any particular product; *get your name out there!*

CONFIRMATION LETTERS—YES OR NO?

Comparably successful producers have diametrically opposite views on the value of appointment confirmation letters.

"I always do confirmation letters," says Shari Halloran who solicits for John Scott in Topeka, Kansas. "Then his secretary calls on the day of the appointment."

But in Portland, Oregon, Bob Beswick says, "I very rarely confirm by mail. It's not worth the time or the postage. I also very rarely confirm by phone; a confirmation contact makes it too easy for them to postpone or cancel. I only confirm if I have to drive more than 20 miles."

In my experience, we rarely confirmed, but often because the appointments were made only a few days in advance, not long enough for anyone to forget, and often with the possibility that there would not be time for a letter to arrive.

However, sometimes we did confirm by mail if it was a potentially big sale, possibly with the appointment set several weeks in advance, with confirmation shortly before as part of the agreement. These letters often emphasized particular selling points which had come up in the phone conversations; thus they became reference documents in case the specific reasons why the prospects had agreed to the appointment grew less clear to them with time.

POSTSALE

"We always follow up sales with a very personal letter," says Paul Poulos, with one agency in Vermont and two in

New Hampshire. "We ask, 'Are you happy with our service?' and 'Do you think there's anything we could have
done better?'"

Also, now—when you've just completed a successful transaction—is an excellent time to ask for referrals.

Birthdays, anniversaries, holidays—special occasions of any kind—are all appropriate opportunities to
renew, through a friendly "hello" by mail, the ongoing good
will in which add-on and referral business through the
years is grounded.

If you have a newsletter, be sure to add your new
client's name to your mailing list.

HAND-ADDRESSED LETTERS MORE LIKELY TO BE OPENED

If you have the time and inclination, studies have shown
that hand-addressed letters are more likely to be opened
than those addressed by machines, although where appropriate your "Requested Material" stamp should be sufficient.

CHAPTER 11

More Auxiliary Support:
Simple Systems

SIMPLE SYSTEMS ARE PRIMARY FOCUS

Simple teleprospecting systems are the primary focus of this chapter, systems to make this aspect of your work considerably more productive and less stressful, but without the complexity and/or expense of more sophisticated alternatives.

MANY SYSTEMS GROUNDED IN
HABIT—CLOSER LOOK NEEDED

Systems are an intrinsic component of everything we do. Everything we do, we do in one way rather than another. I could eat soup with my hands behind my back, or I could use a spoon. The *system, or procedure* of using a spoon is,

177

obviously, considerably more effective than the no-hands approach, although both are perfectly viable.

A lot of what we do, we do by habit; perhaps we thought about it in the beginning, or perhaps it simply evolved, but now we operate pretty much on automatic pilot.

Sometimes, what we do on automatic pilot is terrific. It gets us precisely where we want to go smoothly and quickly, leaving our minds free for far more profound musings. However, sometimes automatic pilot ends up taking us across the street by way of Hong Kong.

STUCK IN OLD PATTERNS

Automatic or not, we all have behavior patterns; some are constructive, while others leave much to be desired. When we stick with a teleprospecting-related behavior pattern which leaves much to be desired, it is generally for one or more of the following reasons:

1. The pattern has become so automatic, to question it never seriously occurs to us; often we don't even realize we're in it.

2. Despite the negatives, it is known—familiar—and it works. The unknown, we fear, could be worse.

3. We balk at the transition itself, the overall disruption, and sometimes expense, of even a relatively minor switch-over process.

4. Even though willing to change, we don't know what to want and/or how to get it.

IMPROVEMENT THROUGH AWARENESS

Much of what follows is an arbitrary synthesis of how I and others have dealt with certain common systems issues. Some of it will fit your needs beautifully; some won't, but if what doesn't nonetheless causes you to question and consequently improve your overall operation, it will have served its purpose.

MONEY RARELY AN ISSUE

Money is rarely an issue in simple systems. More often than not, better mousetraps don't add a penny to whatever you're already spending. Rather, they are created merely by changing how you do whatever you're already doing.

COMPUTERS SOMETIMES HELP, SOMETIMES HINDER

If you have a computer, certainly you will use it as a meat-and-potatoes data base, but in direct connection with direct calling, although some find it a welcome time saver, others find it distracting. If it distracts you, drop it!

I have never used a computer in place of pieces of paper I could move around while calling, nor would I want to try it. File cards, lists, scratch pads, presentation material, maps, appointment calendars, I need each in its own *place*, and what that place is can switch in an instant.

Also, as mentioned earlier, if your whole calling setup is computer based and you decide to bring in an independent, you will be limited to one who can work with your system, which seriously limits your selection.

WITH OR WITHOUT COMPUTERS, CERTAIN HARD COPY NECESSARY

With or without a computer, you will need a *hard-copy* file marked "Teleprospecting." It needs to be hard primarily for easy mobility of documents, and for storage for noncomputer-generated pieces of paper. Also, even with a computer, sometimes hard drives/disks develop problems. Protect yourself!

Some of the hard-copy file contents you will place beside you as you do your own calling, or you will hand to whomever you've hired. The hard-copy file will also contain notes which you did not feel like opening a computer file to copy. And it will contain sales material which you have received from vendors selling anything relative to your operation. Also, if your calling area is large enough that zigzagging to meet your appointment schedule would be more than a minor annoyance, unless you're doing your own calling and know the area very well, your Teleprospecting file needs at least one map.

STEP-BY-STEP-BY-STEP REVIEW/ANALYSIS

I've always been good at packing suitcases. My system is: in my mind, in great detail I go over what I will do, from the moment I arrive. Some is firmly set; some is fluid.

To evaluate what you're already doing, for the purpose of adding, subtracting, and eventually fine-tuning—let's pack! We are not going to "pack" a computer, but many of the pieces of paper we'll use may have been computer generated, and most of the information gathered may eventually be transferred to a computer file, as suits your particular needs.

BEGINNING A DAY IN THE LIFE OF A TELEPROSPECTOR

Although what follows takes the viewpoint of an independent teleprospector, most is equally valid if you do your own calling.

AGENT/INDEPENDENT-TELEPROSPECTOR CONFERENCE

At 8:57 A.M., I walk into the agency reception area. By 9:02, I am in my agent's office. We review:

1. The lead; probably a product or service rather than the agent or agency. But whatever the lead, we focus on what makes it special, with particular attention to

   a. Its *features*. Where is the most pizazz in *how* it works?

   b. What are its *benefits*? What can it *do for* the prospect?

2. If there is a specific script on which I'll be basing my presentation, we review it. I make changes; sometimes major, in this case relatively minor. My agent tells me—very generally, because as I go along I'll fine-tune without him or her based on what works best— whether my changes are

   a. Legal

   b. Comfortable for the agent. I must not promise, even by implication, anything which he or she cannot deliver.

3. We review responses to the objections I'll most likely encounter.

4. I pick up basic information on my agent and the agency. Even without either as my actual lead, I still need to be prepared. Questions most commonly asked about both relate to length of time in the business.

5. He or she gives me special instructions, for example, what questions *require* answers by prospects? If my agent will not be around at the end of the day,

what does he or she want done with calling materials and appointments?

6. My agent gives me his or her schedule and makes clear availability for appointments. I'm told how to reach the agent (or the backup) if I need help during the calling stint and the agent is not in his office. We arrange to meet at the end of the day to discuss results. If I'm there for only one day a week, this is when I should be paid.

By 9:20, I've collected all I need. The meeting went quickly. Sometimes they run considerably longer, especially if we begin with only a basic concept and create a new pitch, or if the product is complex. If you're fortunate enough to have a *really* sophisticated teleprospector, you may want to begin at what is really the beginning and brainstorm on which lead you'll use.

Because of the time spent together today, if I call again on the same project, probably I will not need another meeting before beginning. It will be enough if we merely talk on the phone for a few minutes and I am left the necessary supplies.

ON MY OWN—READY, GET SET!

By 9:25, I'm seated behind my desk in an otherwise empty office down the hall. In front of me, I have

1. *enough names with phone numbers to keep me busy, with plenty left over* (at *least* enough to make 30 calls per hour, even though it's unlikely that I'll make anywhere near that many). Preferably, the list is in the form of stick-on labels. I also have "backup," probably a phone directory, in case the list is "bum."

2. a pitch.

3. special product information, if a special product is to be presented, possibly brochures, along with notes from the conference with my agent. Thus I'm prepared to answer at least some of the questions commonly asked, although my preferred answer always is that my salesperson will do a much better job than I could in providing whatever information the prospect wants, when they meet.

4. *lots* of 5" × 7" file cards, also a file card case with dividers, some by hour, some by month, and some by subject.

5. pens: red and black.

6. my agent's appointment book and, if he or she wants appointments in an area I don't know, a map.

7. assorted forms to collect assorted information.

8. a scratch pad.

9. paper clips/stapler/rubber bands.

10. if my salesperson will be out while I'm calling, either a number where he or she can be reached, or the name of someone else from whom I can get help if I need it.

_____

CLAIM YOUR TELEPHONE DIRECTORY!

I move my list to where I can read it clearly while calling. If it is a phone book *and I have notes in it*, the book itself *has my salesperson's name written in marker on the thickness of the pages*, top, bottom, and front. "Who took my phone book?" comes up far more rarely when the book itself speaks loudly enough as to who really owns it!

If your office has a *serious* directory shortage, by all means, lock yours away, but at the same time, call your telephone company business office and order more. Usually, they're free!

PITCHES/TELEPHONE PRESENTATIONS

Pitches/telephone presentations (the terms are synonymous) will be covered in depth in Chapter 12.

MAJOR TIME SAVER—CODE YOUR RESULTS

As I hang up, I quickly *code* the outcome of each call onto whatever list I'm using. To write out these results, even in abbreviations, is a serious, surprisingly common time waster.

To code, you can use letters, numbers, or symbols. I find symbols easiest, but use whatever feels comfortable. Basically, there are five categories:

1. a *definite appointment* (I use a small solid circle)

2. *strong lead*—probable appointment, but needs more work (I use the outline of a circle, not filled in, which works especially well because it's easy simply to fill it in if/when it changes categories to become an appointment.)

3. *did not reach proper person—try again* (checkmark, possibly with cramped, tiny marginal notes, sometimes with arrows pointing to other parts of the page, on callback time and/or name of contact person)

4. *dead in the water*—absolutely no, forget it (X)

5. *out of date, bum list, waste of time* (line through name)

FORM OF YOUR LIST INFLUENCES BEST WAY TO TRY AGAIN

To hand copy the company name et al. onto a file card merely so you can add the appropriate contact's name and a time when he or she will be available usually takes more time than can be justified by the results. Unless your target market is so narrow that each name is precious, you'll come out ahead spending this same time simply making new calls instead.

TIME AND SPACE MARGINALLY A MESS

Trying to work from marginal notes on a crowded list can also be counterproductive. Marginal notes are often hard to read, squeezed into inadequate space. Also, the *times* to call back will be out of sequence, for example, on page 3, Mr. Smith was to be called at 2:15, while on page 1 (which I'm not looking at anymore, because I'm on page 8, now) is a note that Ms. Jones will be available at noon.

CREATING MORE MANAGEABLE LISTS

If you're using a phone book—or any other list which does not give you adequate space for notes as you go along—you *can* photocopy, shifting and shaping, until you come up with a manageable number of names on one page. "Manageable" means your caller can draw an arrow into blank spaces allowing for fast notes. Nonetheless, it remains cumbersome, and certain callback *time* notes are likely to expire unused in the general confusion.

STARTING WITH MORE MANAGEABLE LISTS

However, if the names are already on individual file cards, or if stick-on labels allow me, in essence, to create printed cards in an instant, I will have a data *form* I can manage far more effectively. I will be able to write whatever I want in enough space and then move the card with the name in with others to be called within the same time frame.

Now, it is far more likely that my immediate information—Mr. X of Company Y will be back at Z time—will not be wasted.

WHEN TO CREATE "CALL-AGAIN" CARDS, WITHOUT PREPRINTED SUPPORT

But without stick-on labels or preprepared file cards, I need more finely tuned criteria. When is creating a card on an "old" call probably worth the time it takes away from "new" contacts?

I invest this time when anyone at the company has said they believe there may be interest. I also do it when "Joe" says, "I don't handle that. Talk to Sam." This probably will get me past Sam's screener. In response to "Who's calling?" I'll answer, *with absolute truthfulness*, "My name's Suzy. Joe said to call Sam." Joe has also given me a *truthful* opening with Sam. "Sam! My name's Suzy. Joe said I should talk to you about this." *This will catch Sam's interest; probably he will at least let me finish the presentation*, which immediately gives me an edge; the call is no longer ice cold.

Just be sure that in the first call, you get Joe's name. Usually I get the name of anyone willing to dialogue with me!

In summary, anything in that first call which you feel may give you an edge in a second call makes preparing a card probably worth the investment.

THE INVISIBLE ADVANTAGE

Because most calls do not turn into appointments, to avoid drowning in time-consuming clerical work if I do not have file cards already containing the basic information I need (as is the case, for example, when I call directly from the phone book) in my initial call, I am as invisible as possible. "Joe handles that, but he's away from his desk," I am told. I respond, "Thanks. I'll try again."

This is perfect. I will try again—because the checkmark on my list has told me to do so. However, because the checkmark is all the information I kept, I won't remember that Joe handles it, but so what? They won't remember me, either. Again, I'll ask who handles the company's benefits; again they'll tell me it's Joe, and maybe this time I'll catch him in.

A checkmark is especially good for this category, because most of those I "call again" will, like the majority, eventually refuse to meet with you, which moves them into the "dead-in-the-water" category, which is coded with an "X." To turn a checkmark into an X, simply draw the extra line through it.

"DEAD IN THE WATER," MAY SWIM AGAIN!

"Dead in the water" rates an X rather than a line through it because if you're feeling creatively obstinate, there's no reason why a *different* teleprospector cannot try these same names again even in the relatively near future. It's not uncommon that another voice will connect with another person or even catch the same one who said "no" in a more receptive mood.

KEEPING TRACK OF BUM LIST ENTRIES

A line through the name is used for bum list entries because, on the scribbled-up pages which lists so often become, I find lines easiest, visually, to count. If you are using a commercially prepared list which you are evaluating for timeliness and accuracy, counting enough cross-outs may earn you a credit and/or motivate you to look elsewhere next time you are in the market for additonal names.

TIME-BASED CALLBACKS—HOURS

I'm wearing a watch. If I didn't have one, I'd need a clock. To accommodate anyone who tells me to call back in 10 minutes or whenever, I need to keep track of the time.

My system is to either lay out in a line or place in hour categories in my file case cards on which, based on my calling results, I will have written "CB" for "call back" after 10:00, after lunch, after 2:00, 3:00, and so on.

Hourly, I check—and call back. In the course of a *full* day, usually I do reach most of the people I set out to reach.

TIME-BASED CALLBACKS—MONTHS

In my file card case, I have another CB category; it is by month. If a prospect shows interest but tells me to call back in a month or so, I write the CB date on the prospect's card and then drop it into the proper CB time slot. In these circumstances, my notes are exceptionally detailed, because memory fades. Also, perhaps I'll be available when it's time to call again, but perhaps, instead, someone else will be relying on what I wrote.

"TRY AGAIN" AND "HARD-TO-REACH" CATEGORIES

In the back of the case, I have two more sections, one marked Try Again and another Hard-to-Reach. Try Again encompasses people I'm simply not connecting with. Perhaps they are chronically away from their desks, in meetings, or whatever.

Normally, I try *no more* than three times to reach those in the Try Again section. After three tries, they are moved from Try Again to Hard-to-Reach. In Phoenix, Arizona, in her teleprospecting classes, instructor Joni Fairbrother quotes as an appointment "hit rate," 1 in 20 calls. For lack of data more specific to whatever particular project you may be working on, 20 at least gives us a baseline. With 20 as a baseline, with each call you make, statistically the odds are 20 to one against you. Therefore, if you call one person 10 times, had you been calling and reaching 10 different people instead, you would be half way to another appointment, while the one person you've called 10 times will *probably* be simply one more "no."

PURSUING "HARD-TO-REACH" PROSPECTS, TO FILL AN APPOINTMENT VOID

However, in the back of the case the Hard-to-Reach group awaits resurrection from its otherwise dusty archive position under one set of circumstances.

If my agent were going to be in area A, with perhaps three or four (or more!) appointments the same day, a last-minute cancellation or a blank spot with no "new" names to call in whatever category we were pursuing could represent a serious waste of time. In this situation, gleaning the hard-to-reach crowd to fill out the schedule could be well worth the investment, especially if out-of-your-immediate-area travel were involved.

LEAVING MESSAGES—BAD IDEA

If by now you're beginning to think leaving messages would be easier, let's review some of the reasons why leaving messages is a bad idea.

Teleprospectors sell sizzle, *very* rarely steak. Most messages become steak only, more often than not as welcome as last week's hamburger, which is why cold calls from insurance salespeople are so rarely returned. Of course you could leave your name without stating the nature of your business, but usually this is not only ineffective, sometimes it actually offends.

Nor are you likely to feel comfortable with even occasional return calls from people whose names you don't recognize. Of course, you could ask them questions to jog your memory, but leaving messages for people you don't even remember when they call back does not make you appear overly professional.

Probably most important, however, is the fact that when you leave a message, *you give up control.* The *power* now rests in the prospect's hands. If you continue to call, you're wide open to, "He has your message; if he wants to talk to you, he'll get back to you," which cannot happen if you've not left your name.

If *occasionally,* under special circumstances, I do leave a message, I write up a file card, with May Call Back in red, which I will specifically point out to my agent before I leave.

SIZE OF FILE CARDS

My file cards are 5" × 7", not 3" × 5". It's better, I've found, to waste space than to try to attach cards to each other; out of pure orneriness, they will come apart the minute you turn your back. Nor does it work well to keep all your information on one card at the price of not being able to read your own squeezed-in handwriting.

BACK UP!

Because, incredibly, appointments get lost, I usually make two copies. Sometimes I photocopy, or sometimes in the salesperson's appointment book I write the name, address, contact person, and phone number, while on the file card, I include the same information but also all other input which might be of value as the salesperson prepares for the meeting.

PENS—THE RED AND THE BLACK, FORGET BLUE

Black gives me the option to photocopy; blue usually reproduces poorly. My form is to write in *red*, in the upper right-hand corner, *Appointment*. I also use red to write the date and *Confirm*, if confirmation was agreed to when the meeting was set, as is often the case with appointments made several weeks in advance. The rest is in black, except for the date and time. Writing the date and time in red makes it stand out: tells the salesperson at-a-glance when he or she is booked.

If the card is not an Appointment card, I still use red to write, in the same space, either Call or Letter.

In short, red tells my salesperson immediately, visually, what *action*—to keep an appointment, to confirm, or to call or write in pursuit of a likely appointment—is needed.

CALL CARDS/LETTER CARDS

A Call card notes serious immediate interest, but tells the agent that another call is needed to turn the interest into an appointment; for example, if the prospect was not at his desk, so could not check his calendar, but a call the next morning should firm it up, or possibly he or she wants a partner to participate in the initial interview, but the partner won't be available until "sometime next week," or more commonly, despite serious interest, a definite appointment hinges on information I could not supply.

OTHER OPTIONS FOR COLLECTING AND PRESERVING DATA

But certainly file cards—or direct computer entry—are not your only options. I've also worked for people who have had different forms for "Appointments" and "Leads," sometimes 8½ "× 11" sheets of paper with blanks to be filled in with specific information. An "Appointment" sheet spells out the time and place, and *whether or not you need to confirm*; remember, you are usually better off if you do *not* confirm.

It also allows ample space for any notes the caller may feel will help you prepare.

A "Lead" may require either a phone call or a letter as the next step. In effect, it says that you probably have an appointment, if appropriate additional action is taken.

KEEP IT BRIEF, KEEP IT SIMPLE

However, as you design your system to record appointments and leads, whatever form that system may ultimately take, don't get carried away by all that blank space! Remember, *if you require too much information from the prospect at this stage, it will cost you appointments that definitely would have turned into sales!*

PATIENCE, PATIENCE! IT PAYS!

Whatever notes you take, write carefully. You are processing a LOT of data. If pushing too hard, even if you are exceptionally conscientious, you can still mix up whether Mr. Smith is with X or Y company, or—you name it. But don't do it; instead, be patient!

NEW PROJECT INITIAL DATA COLLECTION AND EVALUATION

When beginning a new campaign, you'll need more feedback data than will be necessary after you've had more time to discover what does and doesn't work and to fine-tune accordingly. If you're not getting the appointments you expected, or the follow-up sales, then perhaps you need to reexamine and improve your process, but the problem also could be in what you're expecting yourself or your independent teleprospector to accomplish.

At the other end of the spectrum, if you can hardly believe your success, perhaps you need to *raise* your expectations.

The point—the goal—is to establish realistic performance standards. Eventually, this will give you the cost/benefit clarity you'll need in order to decide *before* you spend any sizeable amounts of time/money teleprospecting whether the particular project you'd like to pursue is probably worth the investment.

ZERO IN ON WHAT YOU NEED TO KNOW

To facilitate these goals, when you begin a new campaign, or redesign an old one, you will need more information than otherwise required. For this purpose, you may want to design a form which will give you more data on each call, for example, What specific objections are most common? Or perhaps, as I learned in calling accountants in New York during normal business hours, one *time of day* was better than others.

What do you need for *your* project? Write it up into a form for you or your outsider to work with, but recognize that time spent writing answers to questions is time spent *not* calling. For this reason, and also because you are still to some degree experimenting, your appointment totals at this point will be somewhat lower than you can reasonably expect later on.

"INFORMATION AD INFINITUM"—WHEN TO SAY "WHEN"

However, you need to limit your data collection. Compiling information ad infinitum is expensive overkill. Never underestimate what you can learn in 4 hours; 20 is a gold mine! If you go beyond this, you may want to scale down how *much* information you seek per contact, but it's also a good idea to ask yourself why you are continuing to collect this kind of information at all.

CREATIVE COMMON SENSE SOMETIMES A SUBSTITUTE FOR HARD DATA

If all this sounds a bit "unscientific," it is—and must remain so, until the same kind of really broad-based hard data that has been collected in the regimented area is collected on agents who do their own calling and on independents

THE "FLOWER SYSTEM"—ENHANCING SUPPORT STAFF RELATIONS

Never underestimate the power of those you count on in your office to process your paperwork and to deal with your prospects/clients by phone or sometimes even in person when you are not available. From photocopying lists to preparing and also often even mailing your follow-up letters, staff people are indispensable.

Because what they do is so important to your success, don't hesitate to write memos explaining precisely how you want whatever you need handled, but in my experience, the most important words you can use in a memo to staff people are "please" and "thank you." Flowers, also, go a long way. Folks need strokes. When you acknowledge a job well done, in addition to making the universe a little warmer for all of us, you reinforce the behavior that gave you what you needed.

CHAPTER 12

Scripts and Telephone Presentations/Pitches: Principles and Practice

SCRIPTS DEFINED AND CONTRASTED

A *script* is a telemarketing/teleprospecting tool that tells the caller *precisely* what to say, word for word. A telephone presentation or pitch may include a script, but how tightly the caller sticks to the script is largely optional.

REGIMENTED OPERATIONS USE SCRIPTS

With no exceptions that I'm aware of, teleprospectors in large-scale regimented operations work only from scripts. With few exceptions, even on a smaller scale, the degree of regimentation—the extent to which the caller is required to stick to the script—is proportionate to what callers are paid; the lower the money, the tighter the controls.

WHY STICKING WITH SCRIPTS AT LOWER LEVELS IS IMPORTANT

The controls are tight for a number of reasons. Especially at lower levels, it's likely that most of the thinking necessary for the success of the call was done by someone else; when callers stick with the script, they stick with that someone else's thinking.

Also more so at lower levels, pay is low and turnover is high, meaning that all of your continuity and most of your success hinges on your script. Consequently, your primary investment needs to be in *what* is said, not in who says it; the song, not the singer.

Additionally, to improve your script, you need information on what works and what doesn't. When your calls are alike, collecting the necessary data is easier and faster.

SCRIPTS HELP MINIMIZE "SLIPS"

At any level, callers who use scripts are less likely than are those who don't to lose track of what they cannot say, as limited by both law and the need to avoid promises agents cannot keep.

SUBTLETIES IN WORDING CAN BE CRUCIAL

Certain legal limitations are crucial. A superb example is the following: If you are calling members of XYZ Association, offering members-only discount insurance, *by law*, you cannot say you are calling *from* XYZ, but you *can* say you are calling *in reference* to XYZ.

Although both phrases are equally effective in connecting you with the XYZ member you seek, one is legal, the other is trouble! With any "special" lead, concerns of this nature need attention.

But even with common-as-crabgrass leads such as *"Probably* we can save you money," if the word *probably* is left out, you can still find yourself in trouble.

"PRESENTATIONS" VERSUS "PITCHES"—GEOGRAPHICAL PREFERENCES

In certain parts of the country, the word *pitch* is offensive, suggesting a carnival atmosphere, but in other areas, it is the only commonly accepted term. Consequently, throughout this book, with respect for both "frames of preference," I have used *telephone presentations* or, simply, *presentations* interchangeably with *pitches*. They have exactly the same meaning.

"SCRIPTED CALLS" VERSUS "PITCHES WITH SCRIPTS"

In a telephone presentation, what you say may or may not be written out, may or may not *include* a script *as an optional reference point*, but a presentation is very different from a *scripted call* in that it allows individual callers a far greater degree of freedom to be who they are in support of their objectives.

In other words, the criteria for separating a telephone presentation or pitch from a scripted call is not whether or not you use a script. Rather, it is: *Do you have the script, or does the script have you?*

TELEPROSPECTING PRESENTATIONS PRIMARY FOCUS HERE

Because a script can be a *component* in the larger process of telephone presentations, to encompass both, the primary focus of this chapter is telephone presentations.

And because our dominant overall subject is teleprospecting—seeking *appointments* by telephone—what follows zeros in on teleprospecting presentations or, if you'd prefer, teleprospecting pitches.

START TALKING! BUT WHAT DO YOU SAY?

You are seeking an appointment. You've pulled it together; made the call, gotten through to the right person. For this one golden instant, his or her attention is all yours!

Now what? What are you going to say? And are you going to *read* it, or simply talk?

SCRIPT IT, OR WING IT?

If there is an insurance industry teleprospecting equivalent of the chicken/egg debate, it is: Are telephone presentations more effective when you work with a prepared script or merely from notes?

However, unlike the chicken/egg question, on which I have no opinion, on whether to use a prepared script or notes, I have a very strong opinion. It is: In a telephone presentation, use both!

But allow different circumstances to determine which you use when, and understand those circumstances. Understanding will be the basis for your decisions.

SCRIPTS CAN EASE CALLING PRESSURE

I've never worked in a regimented environment, yet I have *always* used a script *to open a presentation*, allowing myself whatever latitude I needed later to close the appointment.

Most of what I've done has been specialty product calling in which, indeed, use of one particular word or phrase was critically important. Although I *could* have held it in my head, a script freed me; eased some of the tension. It also enabled me to focus more energy on listening to what was going on with the prospect.

TIGHT SCRIPTING CAN SUPPORT SHORTER PRESENTATION

In addition, one of my key selling points on why the prospect should *listen to my presentation* was my promise that it would be brief. To honor that promise, I kept pitches very tight, never saying in two words or even two syllables what could be said in one, but to keep it *this* tight, I needed it in writing, in front of me. Frequently, I specifically asked for "10 seconds of your time." Although it wasn't always 10, often indeed it was!

Of course, in states like Oregon, Georgia, Colorado, or any number of other slower-paced areas, even a full minute might be acceptable; however, teleprospecting calls are still business, not social, and a promise to respect the prospect's time—during both the initial contact and the appointment itself—remains a key selling point.

"PARTIALLY PREPARED SCRIPTS"

The middle ground between talking completely spontaneously and using a script is to work from notes, or as Joni Fairbrother, who teaches teleprospecting in Arizona, describes it, "a *partially* prepared script." She suggests keeping key phrases—for example, "no obligation, free quote, are you happy?"—in front of you.

In Fort Worth, Texas, Suzanna Edwards works without notes *in front* of her, but in her mind, she has a very definite four-point structure, which will be explored in depth later in this chapter. It shapes her material whenever she calls.

SCRIPTS AS BRIDGE TO GOOD SPONTANEOUS CALLING

In Rockford, Illinois, Ned Burns *did* use a script when he first came into the business. "When I started, I was pretty bad," he explains. "But I had a good manager. He told me to use a script *until I got comfortable.* Now, I'm okay without one; I'm good. After you've done it a few thousand times, you get good."

LEAD PRODUCT AND GEOGRAPHICAL LOCATION MAJOR CONSIDERATIONS

However, it's important to note that Ned's approach is: "I have some ideas I'd like to share with you," following a preapproach letter usually pegged on an event, and he lives in a small town in Illinois. He is *not* leading with a specialty product, in which the wording can be nit-pickingly technical, in markets as tough and oversolicited as New York City, Seattle, or Los Angeles.

SCRIPTS SUPPORT HIGH QUALITY IN HIGH-QUANTITY CALLING

In describing why he no longer employs a formal script, Ned uses a key word, *comfortable.*

Although I *could* have worked with only notes— tangible or mental—I was *comfortable* with a script, not only because I was doing primarily specialty product calling, but, I'll admit, after the first few hundred calls on the same product, there were moments when I felt my brain had turned to mush. Under these circumstances, to sound bright and enthusiastic for the next hundred calls, I needed to coast through the rejections riding very much on acting technique, "waking up" only when I found someone interested.

The techniques I used were largely mechanical. Mentally or on the script, I marked pauses, I marked words to be emphasized.

When comparing this to a looser approach, the *quantity* of calling is an important consideration. To sound fresh and enthusiastic for a couple of hours is a respectable accomplishment, but to sustain it for seven or eight straight hours is a whole different ball game. Ned never calls for more than one hour at a stretch; beyond this, he says, he would burn out.

MOST COMMON ARGUMENT AGAINST SCRIPTS IS INVALID

The most common argument *against* scripts at these more sophisticated levels is that the caller will not sound spontaneous, but I'll argue with this.

Although the bottom line is, *go with whatever the caller finds comfortable that works*, to rule out scripts through fear that you won't sound spontaneous is to limit your options unreasonably. A *good* script *well presented* will sound just as spontaneous as presentations which are not scripted.

The difficulty is: what constitutes "good" and "well presented" is not always clear.

SUPERSALESPERSON SEEKS PROSPEROUS PROSPECT

Years ago, in conjunction with a book I had written under the pseudonym "Lynn Davis" on meeting people through personal ads, entitled *The Lynn Davis Guide to Personal Ads*, I led seminars on the same subject. Interestingly, *most* people walked into the seminars believing that a *good* personal ad was clever.

Indeed, sometimes clever ads *were* "good," but sometimes they were terrible. What most people failed to realize was that whether or not an ad was good was actually determined by only one criterion: *Without relying on unreasonable promises, did it draw positive responses from the kind of people the advertiser wanted to meet?*

The same criterion applies to teleprospecting scripts.

"CANNED" VERSUS SELF-CREATED SCRIPTS

I'm going to use very few specific examples. The purpose of this chapter is not to hand you "canned" scripts, no matter how good they might be. Instead, it is to *enable you to create your own.* If you use a canned script—even a very good one—taken from a book like this, you can pretty much bank on it that at least a hundred other salespeople in your area will be calling the same prospects you are calling, using the same script, each of you undermining the potential effectiveness of everyone else.

In addition, in successful teleprospecting through either independents or on your own, *you cannot separate callers from what they say*; what gets the appointment is the *package*. This synthesis of words and personality is an extremely individual process.

However, *most* of the time, good pitches have *very* similar underlying structures. These structures, and other often more subtle techniques for enhancing the effectiveness of what you say, without sacrificing your individual style, can be learned.

SCRIPTED OR SCRIPTLESS, "PITCHING" NEEDS CLEAR GOAL AND STRUCTURE

Scripted or scriptless, from the instant you start talking, you are "pitching" your product and will be more effective if

1. Your *structure* is *clearly* organized.

2. Your *goal* is *sharply* in focus.

FOUR-STEP STRUCTURE

In Fort Worth, Texas, Suzanna Edwards still uses what she learned in a course she took 12 years ago. It divided a teleprospecting call into four basic components:

1. Introduce yourself.

2. Present the *reason* for the call.

3. Present the *benefit* of the call.

4. Close with a choice on *when* (not *whether*) to meet.

Let's take a closer look. *Once, again, geographical considerations come into play.*

What Suzanna offers is classic and excellent. *It is also regional*; it works better in some parts of the country than in others.

As a *reason* for the call, she prefers using a referral name. Without one, she may say she's calling because she does a lot of business with people/businesses similar to the one she's just contacted. In Rockford, Illinois, Ned Burns uses as his "reason" a personal event, such as, a promotion, marriage, or birth of a child.

The *benefit* Suzanna generally offers is that she can save the prospect either time or money, or both, but she particularly emphasizes service. "I take extremely good care of my clients," she says. "Service is the key."

Her *close* is a statement that she will be in the prospect's area on a particular day: Would 10 A.M. or 4 P.M. be better?

Now, however, let's get tough; let's reshape it for New York!

NAMES OF INDEPENDENTS—KEEP IT SIMPLE

If following Suzanna's guidelines, I'll begin by introducing myself. I used "Ellen" Davis rather than "*Lou* Ellen" for a number of reasons. Most people have problems with "Lou Ellen." They might ask me to repeat it, or even spell it, all of which wastes time. Because *I* was not keeping the appointment, my name was not really important, as long as it was in harmony ethnically with the name of my agent.

In addition, I had a life quite separate from the teleprospecting. Using "Ellen" instead of the more distinctive *Lou* Ellen helped me to preserve my boundaries.

MORE ABOUT NAMES

Also on the subject of names, *pronounce the prospect's name correctly*, if at all possible. Names break down phonetically. Probably the most common use I made of my scratch pads (other than doodling) was to write out how the names were *pronounced*. Take a moment before you call. If the name is complicated, break it up in your mind, or if you have a chance to ask, take your time; get the spelling, if you need it.

As for first or last names, I always used last, but I've known teleprospectors who did well using first. I don't like it when strangers call me and use my first name. It suggests they are exercising a closeness to me which, frankly, they haven't earned.

Secretaries were a different ball game. They were almost always first names, but when I asked for their names often *only* their first was what they gave me.

My style for asking was usually, "You've been so helpful. What is your name?"

Of course, because I am a woman, and usually they were, also, a sisterhood component came into play. The secretary's name is particularly important if you're going to need a number of calls to reach your target person.

"Hi, Mary. Is he in yet?" generally worked very well for me on follow-ups.

FINE TUNING FOR TOUGHER MARKETS!

This is your obvious opening, right?

> *Good morning / afternoon / evening or, simply, "Hi."*
> *My name's Ellen Davis, and I'm with Super Duper*
> *Insurance.*

Good, right? Actually, no.

In *my* neck of the woods, where life in general moves so much faster than in most other parts of the country, I look at this and see lots to improve.

In all my years of calling, I don't believe I've ever reached anyone who initially was even remotely interested in my name. What they really wanted was to find out *as soon as possible* why I had called, why I was interrupting whatever else they had planned to do with those few moments they were now spending with me.

However, whoever I might be, the vast majority was *quite* sure it did not want to hear from anyone affiliated with Super Duper—or, actually, any other—insurance company!

Result? *Hang-up. Perhaps* following a courteous cutoff such as "not interested"; perhaps not.

MAKING THE MOST OF YOUR FIRST FEW SECONDS

Now, let's rewrite it, keeping in mind that your first few seconds are critical, if you are to "hook" the prospect's interest.

I'm going to start with "Hi." If your personality is such that you're not comfortable with "Hi"—if, perhaps, you have a more formal disposition and can only feel at home with "Good morning" or its equivalent—then use what you need.

However, my reasons for selecting "hi" extend beyond comfort. "Hi" *takes less time than "good morning,"* which matters because I want to get to the *benefit* fast, *very fast!*

My next sentence does not include my name. Nor does it include the word "insurance" or "financial services," an often equally deadly term. Instead, if at all possible, I will *take the name of the agency, and follow it with the word "company."*

We now have, "Hi. I'm with the Jones and Johnson Company."

Immediately move to *benefit*. "We specialize in cutting taxes and other costs for small businesses like yours. There is no charge for our services."

By now, you have probably cut your hang-up rate by about 60 percent. You may not *keep* them on the line long enough to say everything you'd like to say, but so far, they're still with you. And you haven't even given your name yet!

Now give your name.

HANGING ON BY LETTING GO!

The next stage can be handled in a number of different ways.

I *give up control*. I open the door for the prospect to talk. The result is interesting. Wary, suspicious New York consumers whose defenses went up the instant they realized I probably was selling something have *had their power acknowledged*.

I often ask, "Can I have 10 seconds of your time?" *It is disarming*. It tells them I value their time; I have admitted I realize that they can either talk to me or cut me off. But at the same time, it introduces a light tone. Many times, prospects have answered, "Okay—I'm counting." Or, they'll respond, "Not now," thereby opening the door for me to request, "When?" which very often places the name in a callback time slot.

KEEP IT AWKWARD, KEEP IT REAL

And I use "can" instead of "may," because even though "can" is grammatically incorrect, it's more in line with how most people talk. I want my sentences to sound as natural as possible: simple, short, and slightly awkward.

ALTERNATIVES TO "10 SECONDS"

Sometimes other callers (especially men) have told me they would be uncomfortable with the "10 seconds" phrase. "Do you have a minute or so?" is a valid substitute, although I have never found it nearly as effective as "10 seconds."

But *ask*. Often it is the only way you'll really get their attention; without it, too often they remain so wrapped up in figuring out how to get rid of you, they won't really hear you at all.

Most *will* give me 10 seconds.

And usually it's going to take more than 10, but well under 60.

Do *not* ask: "Is this a good time for you?" *This can suggest that you need more than a few minutes*, which the prospect may be reluctant to give you. It also can enmesh you in callbacks in cases where, if you'd asked for only a few seconds, you could have made your pitch *and gotten the appointment* immediately.

PULLING IT ALL TOGETHER

Let's put it together. Also, please note, I have written it out in all capital letters. Perhaps other forms exist, but the only copy I've ever seen to be read on radio or TV shows has been in caps, in the belief that this makes it easier to read out loud.

"SAVE MONEY" SMALL-BUSINESS PITCH

HI. I'M CALLING FROM THE SMITH AND JONES COMPANY. WE SPECIALIZE IN CUTTING TAXES AND OTHER COSTS FOR SMALL BUSINESSES (LIKE YOURS). THERE IS NO CHARGE FOR OUR SERVICES.

MY NAME IS ELLEN DAVIS. CAN I HAVE ABOUT 10 SECONDS OF YOUR TIME?

OKAY. (OR, THANK YOU.) WE CAN PROBABLY SHOW YOU HOW TO CUT YOUR MEDICAL COVERAGE COSTS WITHOUT REDUCING BENEFITS; HOW TO PUT ASIDE TAX-*FREE* MONEY FOR YOURSELF, ALONE, THROUGH YOUR COMPANY;

HOW TO CUT ADMINISTRATIVE COSTS, ACROSS THE BOARD.

ONE OF OUR REPRESENTATIVES WILL BE IN YOUR AREA ON _____.

WHAT I'M ASKING FOR IS ABOUT 15 MINUTES FOR YOU TO SIT DOWN WITH HIM(HER) AND EXPLORE WHAT WE MIGHT BE ABLE TO DO FOR YOU. WOULD _(TIME)_ BE GOOD FOR YOU, OR WOULD _(TIME)_ BE BETTER?

EMPHASIZE TIME LIMIT

Note the emphasis on time; I'll only need 10 seconds to pitch you, and the appointment will require only 15 minutes—unless, of course, it will actually require considerably more. P&C business appointments generally require at least a solid half hour, but potential clients usually already know this.

OTHER OPENINGS

There are, of course, *many* ways to open. "The more unusual your opening line, the better your chances," advises Joni Fairbrother, the Phoenix-based Independent Insurance Agents and Brokers of Arizona teleprospecting instructor.

One of the best opening lines I ever heard, strictly as an attention-getter, came from Shari Halloran, in Topeka, Kansas. Shari's forte is setting up personal life insurance sales appointments for one agent, who employs her full time. His name is John Scott. For me, much of the charm in Shari's opening is in the fact that Shari seemed oblivious to just how original it was.

"Hi," she begins. "My name's Shari Halloran. I'm John Scott's business manager."

Okay—I'll bite. *Who is John Scott?* His *business manager?* Why is this complete stranger having his business manager call me?

As she answers, I'm still listening; I'm still off balance. And then, there was the agent, who shall be nameless, in a state which shall remain unidentified, who, like Shari, focuses on personal L&H. "Good afternoon," he opens. "My name is _____. We locate and train people for upper management positions. Would you be interested in a career change, if the money was right?"

Following through on this theme, he sets up an appointment.

"Yes, it works," he answered. "Quite commonly, I end up with either a new agent trainee or a customer." However, in New York, I suspect far more people would be angry, rather than receptive.

My most common openings centered on an intriguing benefit. Remember the Section 125 Cafeteria Plans? The script I was handed was good, but the following is what eventually evolved; it broke the sound barrier on appointments.

SECTION 125 CAFETERIA PLAN

HI. I'M WITH SUPER DUPER SERVICES.

WE HAVE SOMETHING—IT'S BASED ON AN IRS PROVISION—THAT COSTS YOU NOTHING, CUTS YOUR PAYROLL TAXES, AND RAISES YOUR EMPLOYEES' TAKE-HOME PAY.

MY NAME IS _____ . HAVE YOU GOT ABOUT 10 SECONDS?

You bet they had 10 seconds! This was an especially rewarding product, because a scaled-down version told screeners what was in it for them, as employees whose take-home pay would be raised.

BUSINESS P&C

Here, you have less to play with. Rayda Roundy, in Vista, California, does very well with, quite simply, "My name is Rayda, with El Camino Insurance Agency. Do you accept quotes on your liability and business insurance when it comes up for renewal?"

Your "edge" is in the agency's reputation, sometimes in a price advantage, or in your ability to convince the prospect that your service is superior, which is often tied to the length of time the agency has been in business.

Many of those I interviewed emphasized specialization in a particular kind of business, but Bob Beswick in Portland, Oregon, makes the very valid point that this can backfire.

"Companies in the same business are competitors. Perhaps a client I already have has a bad relationship with the one I'm calling. In a tightly knit business community, as it is here in Portland, emphasizing specialization in a particular area means you service your new prospect's competitors; the company you're calling may decide not to trust you.

"If they pressure me, I'll tell them who else I work with; but I'm not going to volunteer it."

PERSONAL P&C

As explained earlier, teleprospecting for *personal* P&C is not common, *except* when whatever appointments it might glean are intended as doorways to larger sales, usually in the L&H area.

PLAN "A" AND PLAN "B"

Thus far, we've focused on leads aimed at a relatively high entry level. But plan B markets can also pay your rent/mortgage.

Here, cross-category or "hybrid" marketing is a powerful option.

ADVANTAGES FOR P&C/L&H TEAMS

Karen Placek, president of Telephone Marketing Promotions, Inc., the Casselberry, Florida-based teleprospecting firm, offers the following advice: "There are three kinds of insurance which everyone needs," she begins. "Home, auto, and health."

Of course, this assumes the prospect owns a home and auto. If they do, but aren't insured for them or if they don't have health insurance, "they're nervous," she says.

These products lend themselves exceptionally well to a teleprospecting approach. They are clear, easy to present, cut across a very broad market segment, and have definite emotional appeal. Also, they dip into both categories. Car and home are personal P&C, while health is, of course, L&H.

However, not everyone *does* own a car or a home, and many already have at least some health coverage, usually through their jobs or unions or affiliations with other organizations, which does not mean they're inaccessible. It merely means you're going to have to reach *these* people in some other way, all of which brings us back to square 2. If *your* products can't open the door, in a cross-category association, perhaps your partner's can!

These pitches are generally very simple:

SAVE MONEY ON CAR INSURANCE

HI. I'M CALLING ABOUT YOUR CAR INSURANCE. PROBABLY WE CAN SAVE YOU SOME MONEY.

MY NAME IS _____ , AND I'M WITH SUPER DUPER INSURANCE. HAVE YOU GOT A MINUTE?

WE'D LIKE TO SIT DOWN WITH YOU FOR ABOUT 15 MINUTES AND SEE WHAT WE CAN DO FOR YOU. ONE OF OUR AGENTS IS GOING TO BE IN YOUR AREA NEXT _____ . WOULD YOU HAVE SOME TIME, AROUND _____ , OR WOULD __(ANOTHER DAY)__ AT __(ANOTHER TIME)__ BE BETTER?

THE FINE ART OF "DELIBERATE AMBIGUITY"

This opening illustrates an important point: the fine art of *deliberate ambiguity*. You win the prospect's immediate attention by *implying* that you are associated with the insurance carrier they already have, which is not true, but neither are you lying. Another example of this appeared in the last chapter, in connection with legal boundaries; under certain circumstances, you are calling *in reference to*, rather than *from*, but the *impression* is "from."

Frankly, this never bothered my conscience; *in reference to* was what got their attention, but once they'd given it, an extraordinarily high percentage were delighted to make the appointment. And very possibly you *can* reduce car insurance premiums. Especially if this is one of your major door-openers, let's hope you really do have exceptional expertise on the subject.

KEY PHRASES/CONCEPTS IN PRESENTATIONS

But whatever your approach, keep in mind the classic key phrases/concepts presented here:

1. You have *ideas* to share ("idea" is a powerful buzzword).

2. *Are you happy* with your present coverage/cost/service?

3. *Free*/no-charge/no-obligation *service*, in the form of an *examination*/audit/review of present needs and/or existing policies.

4. *Reduce premiums*, with no reduction or possibly even an increase in coverage.

5. *Accumulate money* in savings.

6. *Protection*—take care of you/your family (but be wary of long-term disability as a lead; most people are reluctant to believe a medical catastrophe could really happen to *them*; straight medical is better).

7. *Special expertise* (through heavy experience in a particular area, or possibly with an offbeat lead product, and/or through computers which enable you to examine more possibilities, and/or affiliation with an unusually large number of companies, enabling you to "shop around" more effectively than your competitors).

8. An extension of the foregoing, but important enough to be listed separately, *special expertise on tax laws* can greatly enhance the *cut taxes* approach.

9. Superior *service*.

COLD CALLING AND KINGS—MASTERING THE CHESS CONNECTION

However, whatever your product or approach, by definition, *teleprospecting* is the process of seeking *appointments* with *prospects* by *telephone*. The key word here is *appointments*.

Do you play chess? In case you don't, it is an intricate two-player board game in which widely differentiated pieces are moved in individual patterns, but the outcome is determined by only one piece; you win when you capture the other player's king. Frequently, beginners at chess lose track of this. They get caught up in capturing other pieces, or guarding their own or through any one of a number of other distractions, they lose sight of the real objective—just as so many beginning teleprospectors lose sight of what teleprospecting is really about.

When you teleprospect, your "sale" is the appointment; your "close" occurs in the instant in which a definite meeting time and place are established.

All else exists only to support this instant!

Yet *losing sight of the close is the single most common problem I've discovered in training people over the years*, whether they are agents or independents.

Sometimes agents especially get caught up in beginning to sell, or sometimes either independents or agents succumb to friendly dialogue, occasionally even on subjects that have nothing to do with insurance.

And sometimes, in spite of all this, they make appointments—*but not nearly as many as could reasonably be expected if their goal were properly focused!*

CHAPTER *13*

Objections!

If you're relatively new to teleprospecting, some of what follows may seem glib. However, if you've really been there, as I have, you will realize that *this is reality.*

ARTIFICIAL AND REAL OBJECTIONS

Objections fall into two categories: artificial and real. Artificial objections are not authentic; what you're hearing is entirely different from what's actually going on. Real objections are honestly presented genuine reasons why prospects do not want to see you; what you're dealing with is clear. Although certain specifics on how to deal with both artificial and real objections sometimes vary geographically, *the objections themselves are universal.*

218

ARTIFICIAL OBJECTIONS

Wherever you live, recognizing artificial objections can help you to work past them, but seeing them for what they are can be tricky, because very often they appear to be perfectly valid.

Behind artificial objections is usually one or more of the following sentiments:

1. I don't like you.
2. I don't trust you.
3. I don't believe you; you'll waste my time.
4. You've caught me at a bad time; I don't even want to think about it now, nor do I want to think about when I *will* want to think about it.
5. I'm not happy, but I'm so sick of the whole subject, I don't *care* if you have a better mouse trap; it's not in me to go over it one more time.

FIELDING ARTIFICIAL OBJECTIONS— POINTS 1 THROUGH 3

Points 1 through 3—I don't like, trust, or believe you; you'll waste my time—are frequently difficult to distinguish from each other.

Point 1—being disliked—can be specific or generic. Perhaps the person you've reached has a fantasy of drowning all telephone solicitors, and you happen to fall into that category, or perhaps, indeed, there is something in your style which whomever you're speaking to finds abrasive.

Listening can help you. If your prospect seems overly cold or abrupt, *maybe* disliking you is the issue. If so, sometimes you can adjust your style to defuse what you're hearing, for example, if you've come on strong, you can tone it down, or—more commonly an issue with points 2 and 3—if you've lost credibility by promising the moon, perhaps you can qualify the offer, *even if you really do have the moon in the palm of your hand.*

However, with one exception, living with these three artificial objections is a fact of life, and the most important thing you can do is make peace with it; accept it as perfectly natural and not become discouraged.

THE ONE EXCEPTION

The one exception is, if you run into these particular objections an inordinate percentage of the time, perhaps something in your presentation needs a closer look. Here, input from friends/family/business associates can be invaluable. Or, if you're feeling especially courageous and if it fits your personal style, perhaps you can actually ask a few prospects: "If I've offended you—how? I'd really appreciate it if you could tell me." Not only can this, when handled right, sometimes give you valuable information, it can also be disarming. Even in New York, even in business situations, strangers are often far more generous spirited than we tend to expect.

FIELDING ARTIFICIAL OBJECTIONS— POINTS 4 AND 5

The last two hurdles—in one form or another, simply not wanting to deal with it—crop up most often when you are talking to the top person in the company, whose strength/talent/primary interest is in marketing rather than in the financial end of the business, but they are also common with personal insurance.

POINT 4

The best way to field the *unspoken* no-time issue is to *anticipate it and build your defenses into your pitch*, which is precisely what you are doing when you ask for only a few seconds or minutes to talk, and emphasize that the appointment itself will also be brief.

A *spoken* time issue is easier, because you can deal with it directly; you can focus on it with a clarity not really possible when the prospect is actually saying, "We're happy with what we have," or any number of other *artificial* go-away tactics.

POINT 5

I can't stand thinking about it anymore is more difficult, because it's less rational. *If* this is what's going on, you can respond by saying you're glad they're happy, you understand that they have no money or whatever, but with their permission, you'll call back in three to six months. If they agree, it gives you an opening when you do call back; if they don't, it doesn't matter. Unless you are operating in a *very* small town, you can call again anyway or (often better) have someone else do it for you, making no reference to the previous call.

The point is, most of us get stressed out sometimes, but we pull out of it; we heal. So wait. Give it time. Even if you could get the appointment now, seeing someone who's so shut down on the subject that they're not likely to listen to you seriously anyway wastes everybody's time.

REAL OBJECTIONS

In Laurel, Mississippi, Mike Axton lists the four *real* personal insurance cold-call objections he finds most common:

1. I have insurance at work.
2. I don't have money.
3. I don't have time.
4. I have a brother in the business.

I'll add others, collected elsewhere, including some from my own experience. Still in the personal arena, we have

5. What I already own is enough.

In the business world, numbers 2, 3 and 4 still apply, but we also have

6. The union takes care of it.
7. My accountant takes care of it.
8. Even if your price *is* somewhat lower, the price we have is *okay,* and we're happy with the service.

"STALLS" SOMETIMES MEAN NO

Not *exactly* "objections," but broadly in the same category because they are presented as reasons for not meeting with you, we have "stalls," which may or may not be valid. They include

9. Send information. If I'm interested, I'll call you.
10. *Sometimes,* "not for at least six months" (or when-ever) is invalid; it really means, "no."

REGIONAL DIFFERENCES INFLUENCE STYLE IN HANDLING OBJECTIONS

How much time you'll have to deal with objections usually varies widely geographically. In certain parts of the country—especially the South, especially when the prospect is a "southern gentleman" and the teleprospector a "lady"— dialoguing frequently does run longer than in most New York teleprospecting calls.

Other specific areas also march to the beat of a slower drummer. "It's much easier out here," says insurance salesman Randy Crawford, first mentioned in Chapter 3. Randy is an expatriate Easterner now living in Fort Collins, Colorado. "The Midwest is laid back. In the East, it's all very factual; 'don't hug me, just give me the information.'"

But nothing here is intended to overcategorize by state; even in basically fast-paced states, often small towns are slower.

HOW TO ARGUE IS UNIVERSAL — HOW MUCH IS REGIONAL

The *content* of what follows is valid for fielding objections anywhere, but you'll need regional adjustments. For example, in Manhattan, if a prospect requested information by mail, usually I'd push for the appointment, instead. Yet in many parts of the country, sending information would be appropriate. In slower-paced areas, often the whole *process* is slower, from more time/money invested in laying the groundwork through preapproach mailings, through far more laid-back dialoguing, on through accepting "no" or at least, "not right now," far more readily.

"SCRIPT" FORMAT USED TO ENHANCE CLARITY

Nothing here is intended as a *rigid* "script." The *content* is what's important, but the content is presented in an example format rather than in summary, because over the years, I have found examples more helpful in teaching this kind of material.

SALESPERSON'S VIEWPOINT ADAPTABLE BY OUTSIDERS

Although formatted for salespeople doing their own calling, others can easily adapt what follows.

PERSONAL INSURANCE

Most common objections to personal insurance are *somewhat* different from commercial, although many of the principles are the same. This section focuses on fielding *personal* insurance teleprospecting objections, but much of what follows is also applicable to commercial lines.

"I Have Insurance at Work"

Salesperson   Yes, most people do, which is why what we offer is designed to supplement existing coverage. The trouble with insurance through your job is, most people don't find out where the holes are until it's too late.

"IDEAS" IS A POWERFUL BUZZWORD—USE IT!

I have some ideas on filling those holes I'd like to discuss with you. But maybe what you already have *is* adequate; let's find out. I'll be happy to go over it with you. Answer any questions. If you *do* have everything you need, at least you'll know.

"NO CHARGE, NO OBLIGATION, FREE!"

There's no charge, no obligation.

Prospect If you're not expecting to sell me something, why do you want to see me?

Salesperson Because if I do this for you, when you *do* want to buy something, I hope you'll think of me. Or maybe you'll recommend me to someone else.

GO FOR THE CLOSE
(emphasize time limit)

You'll probably be surprised by how much we can cover in 15 minutes.

Prospect I don't believe you'll take only 15 minutes.

Salesperson No, sometimes it is only 15 minutes. Sometimes not, but if it does run longer, it'll be because you want it to, because you have enough questions to keep both of us busy. Look—15 minutes is your only commitment. I'm going to be in your area, anyway. How about next Wednesday at six, or would Thursday at seven be better?

Prospect Well—okay. Thursday.

After the main issue is settled—the prospect has agreed to see you—make sure the spouse will be there!

"I Don't Have Money"

Salesperson That's one of the reasons I called. Everybody has trouble saving money. I specialize in long-range programs for saving—accumulating—money. I'm really very good at it. I have some ideas I'd like to share with you.

"I Don't Have Time"

Do *not* start describing the horrors of a crisis made worse by inadequate coverage! You want appointments, not people who resent you for making them feel inept/irresponsible.

Salesperson   I can certainly understand that! I don't have much time, either. So let's go ahead and set something up, even if it's three or four weeks from now. We can confirm a day or so in advance, if you'd like, but this way, we'll both reserve the time. This is important, you know; insurance requirements change. At some point, you do need to update. I have some ideas I'd really like to share with you.

"I Have a Brother in the Business"

Or, as Mike Axton's brother-in-*law* used to say, "I have a brother-in-*law* in the business." Or a cousin, father, wife—you name it. "I'm happy with the broker/agent I already have" also falls into this general category.

Here, of course, you're fishing. If the prospect *really* buys only from someone else, indeed, do you want the appointment?

Salesperson   Great! Have you talked to him, lately?

Prospect   Last week.

Salesperson   Great! But why not take a look at what I have, anyway? Check up on your brother; make sure he's taking care of you as well as he should. I have some ideas that might be different from his; I'd like to share them with you. Won't cost you anything; takes only about 15 minutes.

"I Already Own Too Much!"

Salesperson   That's certainly possible. But, you know, sometimes you can reduce your cost without reducing coverage—or expand the coverage you already have, for the same price. What's available changes constantly.

But even if cost or coverage aren't issues, is the way you have it set up saving you every penny possible on taxes? Every year, tax laws change.

MEETING INITIALLY WITH ALL PRINCIPALS IS NOT ALWAYS POSSIBLE

As you want the spouse present when meeting with a prospect for personal insurance, when you first meet with a business prospect, certainly you would *like* to have all principals present, but often this group can be prohibitively difficult to assemble.

I have never pushed to have all principals present. Here, as elsewhere, the tenuousness of a teleprospecting connection comes into play. You may have to prove yourself through an initial contact with only one; if it goes well, the rest follows.

But sometimes the *prospect* will want his partner/accountant/you-name-it to participate in the first meeting. The downside is, you may need to really stay on top of it to make sure they don't all simply give up!

"The Union Takes Care Of It"

You *could* pursue the union itself, but union sales through an initial teleprospecting connection are as unlikely as corporate sales.

Salesperson   I realize that. I'm looking for the owner.

Prospect   I'm the owner.

Pitch a special product; tax savings are generally good.

Salesperson   We do a lot of work with owners; we've saved them a lot of money. We also help them hang on to nonunion key employees. In fact, we have a way, under the new tax laws—

"My Accountant Takes Care Of It"

Salesperson Wonderful! We work with a lot of accountants. Frankly, we've shown many of them ways to save taxes for their clients that they didn't even know existed. Let's set a time when he or she can be there, or would you rather I ran it by him or her first? Initially, we'll need only about 15 minutes. What's his/her name?

"Even If Your Price Is Lower, We're Happy With What We Have"

This is most common in the P&C area, where close contact through ongoing service is a major issue. If prospects are happy with the service—especially if they've been burned by bad service in the past—you're in a tough position. You *can* use

Salesperson Certainly I can understand your feelings, but you know, insurance needs do change; it's a good idea every now and then to get a second opinion. We'd like to give you one. No charge. If you still don't want to switch, no problem. On the other hand, if we are low enough, we have an excellent reputation for service. Maybe you'll decide you are interested.

If you've been in business long enough for it to be a plus, add

We've been in business X years, and we've still got most of the clients we started with, which speaks for itself on service.

Let's at least meet and discuss it. Is next Tuesday at ten good for you, or would Wednesday at two be better?

But because the relationship involves heavy ongoing contact, a satisfied customer is still a difficult prospect. In Vista, California, Rayda Roundy introduces herself and then asks, quite directly: "Do you accept quotes when your insurance comes up for renewal?" If "yes," she pursues it; if "no," she moves on to the next call.

"Send Information"

Prospect Well—maybe. Send me some information.

Maybe this is a brush-off—but maybe not. If you're not sure, go fishing! If it's not a brush-off, probably they will not object if you keep control. Therefore, tell them you'll call again.

Salesperson Okay. I'll get it off to you today, and call you again within the next week or so, after you've had a chance to read it. Thanks a lot.

If they object—"don't call us, we'll call you," *probably* I would not send it; the decision would depend on the cost, in both time and money.

But, remember, these are *cold* calls. When someone who is already a client requests information, by all means, follow through!

Now, however, let's argue; let's go for it!

Prospect Send me some information, okay?

Salesperson Well, I *could*, but frankly

Choose one of the following: both together can be overkill.

1. There are so many variables in each particular case, what you'd need would be as thick as a phone directory!

2. If you're not familiar with the material, it can seem awfully technical.

We're talking about only 15 minutes (or 1/2 hour minimum with most P&C business cases). Any questions you might have can be answered immediately. I'm going to be in your area anyway—how about 2:00, next Wednesday?

"NOT NOW — MAYBE IN SIX MONTHS"

If you're calling for P&C, obviously ask for their X-date. If calling for anything else, the name of the person you spoke to goes into the appropriate time slot in your callback file. Always get the name. If it's difficult to pronounce, write it out phonetically. If it's a potentially important client, you might want to send a thank-you-for-your-time letter; this gets your name in front of them, in writing. You might also want to send another letter, perhaps a week or so before you actually do call back.

BOBBING AND WEAVING AROUND WHETHER YOU'RE SELLING INSURANCE

Often these issues come up when your approach is a not-quite-specified no-obligation financial service, for example, the "save money" small-business pitch presented in the last chapter.

Prospect   Are you selling insurance?

Salesperson   Insurance recommendations are one of our services; it's not all we do.

Or, sometimes you'll run into

Prospect   If there's no charge for any of this, how do you make your money?

Salesperson Well, if you accept any of our recommendations, we *hope* you'll buy through us, but there's no obligation—

Here, *immediately*, as always, go for the close!

SCREENERS!

Screeners can knock you out of the ballpark before the game even begins. If you feel this is happening, you have two options. You can fight it through, or you can walk away, move on to the next call.

I suggest you seek a balance. If you find you're spending far too much time arguing, and not enough calling, then probably you need to let go sooner. On the other hand, if you rarely argue, perhaps you need to retest your limits, possibly experimenting with some of the tools offered in this section.

SCREENERS USUALLY NOT DIFFICULT

But r-e-l-a-x; beware of falling into a paranoid mind-set! *Usually*, when a "screener" says, "What is this in reference to?" their interest is merely informational. Mr. Jones doesn't know you; he wants some sense of what's going on before he picks up his phone.

WHEN SCREENERS ARE DIFFICULT

If they *are* authorized to get rid of you if *they* don't like what they're hearing, you have several options, but there is one option you do *not* have, ever!

You do not have the option to lie. Do not say you are a personal friend of the prospect, do not say you are from the IRS (yes, it's been done!), do not say it is "personal" *if it isn't* (sometimes it is, for example, if you're calling someone at work about personal insurance).

There is good reason for this; indeed, you'll get past the screener—*to a very annoyed prospect! However,* deliberate ambiguity is different. It is a loophole!

If you have the kind of sensitive disposition which would give you no peace if you ever bent a rule, skip this next section. Move on down to *Point-Counterpoint—Standard Screening Responses.*

DELIBERATE AMBIGUITY REVISITED

Still with me? I suspected you might be! The difference between a deliberately ambiguous statement and a lie is, if you are caught, you can wiggle out of a deliberately ambiguous statement with your dignity—*and sometimes your relationship with the prospect*—still intact.

EXAMPLE

An excellent example relates to a call I made to an association member *in reference to* his association, although I was actually calling from an insurance agency.

When I pitched him, the prospect was angry. "You told my secretary you were from my association," he exploded. "You *lied!*"

"No, sir," I answered with icy indignation, "that is not what I told your secretary. I said I was calling *in reference to* the association—specifically as a follow-up to the letter they sent you on the new discount insurance rates being offered to their members by Super Duper Insurance. I'm sorry your secretary misunderstood, but she did."

I was right. The fact that I knew perfectly well she'd misunderstand and, consequently, put me through to him was irrelevant. No, in this case, I did not get the appointment. But *most* of the people with whom I used this approach were not angry at all.

OTHER DELIBERATE AMBIGUITY EXAMPLES

In the same ballpark is, "I'm calling about his or her taxes," if your basic approach is saving tax dollars. Okay, it sounds like you could be from the IRS, and *I* couldn't do it, but others have, and quite successfully.

It also often works to say, "I'm calling about his/her/your insurance." It can *sound* as though you are with their present carrier, perhaps calling to iron out a problem, *but that's not what you said.*

Of course, all this comes into play only if you are challenged. All you ever *volunteer* to a screener is your name and, only when necessary, the name of your company.

POINT-COUNTERPOINT—STANDARD SCREENING RESPONSES

The following are not at all ambiguous and generally work quite well.

Screener   What is this in reference to?

PERSONAL OR BUSINESS

Salesperson   I'm with the XYZ Company. We specialize in cutting taxes. There is no charge for our services. Is he/she in, or would it be better if I called back later? How about _____ , or would _____ be better?

There is more in this than is probably immediately apparent. The point of focusing so quickly on when to call back is not so much to obtain information as to *deflect* interest in what you want. The focus then becomes Mr. Smith's schedule.

Also, in most cases, *when you run into tighter screeners*, their primary job is to protect the boss *from salespeople*. Saying immediately that there is no charge often disarms.

If it doesn't, you can try:

I'd be happy to explain it in detail, but it's long and rather technical. Really, I do think Mr. Smith will agree that it's important. (We work with a lot of _____ name the company's line of business _____.) If he's busy now, how about if I call back around _____?

Screener   Leave your number. We'll call you.

Salesperson   He wouldn't be able to reach me because I'm making a lot of outgoing calls; I'm having the switchboard merely take messages. I don't mind calling again. Do you think he'd be free in about another half hour, or should I try after lunch?

BUSINESS ONLY

I'm with the XYZ Company. We work with employers *to increase employee benefits* without it costing either the employer or employees any more money.

In short, never underestimate the power of enlightened self-interest!

DODGING THE ISSUE BY DODGING THE SCREENERS

Of course, if it still doesn't work and you're feeling persistent, you can always call back when the screeners are less likely to be there, usually very early in the morning or at lunchtime.

CHAPTER 14

Hanging in Through the Hang-ups!

THE OWL AND THE CENTIPEDE

Once upon a time, a centipede with chronically sore feet paid an owl a lot of money for advice.

"No sweat," said the owl. "Turn yourself into a stork. Then, when you stand, usually it'll be on only one foot; the rest of the time, you'll be flying or parked on a nest."

"Fantastic!" cried the centipede. "How do I do that?"

"Well, actually," answered the owl, "I haven't a clue. I'm a *what* consultant; I never really got into *how*."

"HOW" IS CRUCIAL!

I'm frequently reminded of this story when I see books for salespeople advising them to be positive, cheerful, and so on, but make no mention of *how*. *How*, in light of the thousand natural shocks teleprospectors are heir to, is every bit as important as any other dimension of the process.

BECOMING "OKAY" WITH YOUR FEELINGS

Attitudes reflect feelings. Of course, you *can* "fake it 'til you make it." You can *will* an attitude, otherwise known as "act as if." The philosophy behind this approach is that if you "bring the mind, the feelings will follow," which, *sometimes*, is true.

But this hypothesis approaches the problem from the outside in, which I'm not criticizing. Aside from mood-altering substances, I'll support anything that works. If this works for you, by all means keep it as *one* option, *part* of your complete tool set. However, on balance, I believe that "inside jobs" are more effective and lasting. *Most* of the tools I recommend are in this second category.

Your goal, succinctly stated, is to become "okay" in relation to your *feelings*, in relation to teleprospecting.

"OKAY" DEFINED

"Okay" does not mean you will suddenly view teleprospecting with nothing but unbridled enthusiasm; it does mean that less of it will bother you, less often, and to a lesser degree in both intensity and duration.

FACILITATING YOUR OWN TRANSFORMATION

Transformation in this area is an ongoing process. However, the good news is, there's a lot you can do—probably far more than you realize—to facilitate immediate positive change, *inner* change, at the deepest levels.

Specifically, even if your basic attitude is not really negative, you can still probably substantially improve it by, in no particular order of importance,

1. Improving your actual teleprospecting skills
2. Making your physical surroundings more supportive
3. Avoiding "crutches"
4. Understanding *resistance*
5. Understanding *rejection*
6. More clearly understanding yourself, others, and your relationship with these others within the teleprospecting framework
7. Acknowledging the importance of and remaining open to ongoing exploration of specific emotional support tools.

EMOTIONAL ADVANTAGES IN IMPROVING YOUR ACTUAL SKILLS

Remember how scary it was, in school, when you hadn't done your homework? "Homework" in teleprospecting has been especially difficult, because so much of the training has left so much to be desired. But now, simply the fact that you have tools you probably didn't have before can make a substantial difference in how you *feel*, as you sit down to pick up the phone. Your enhanced success will also help!

SUPPORTIVE PHYSICAL SURROUNDINGS

In Chapter 9, we discussed emotional advantages of a special *place* from which to call, a place in which you will be free of associations with other activities, thus allowing your psyche to, in effect, draw fresh patterns on a comparatively clean sheet of paper.

If your space setup prevents you from doing this, you can still clear the area from which you are calling of all other projects while you call. Of course you'll know they're there, but if you don't actually see them, probably they will be easier to ignore—at least for awhile.

It's commonly recommended that you work from a desk with nothing on it except your immediate teleprospecting materials; "nothing" includes food or drink.

Granted, drinks can spill and leave rings. However, I always had something to drink, usually diet soda with lots of ice. I knew the moment I sat down that I was going to do a *lot* of talking. When I talk that much, my throat gets dry.

BEWARE OF "CRUTCHES"

But I *never* had with me anything even slightly alcoholic or sugary, nor did I ever have anything to munch. Smoking while calling is also a bad idea.

The problem is not how any of these substances might affect one isolated session. Rather, the issue is *conditioning*, the danger of becoming *emotionally dependent* on something—anything—beyond yourself in order to make that next call.

I must confess, my "dry throat" is to some degree a rationalization. The truth is, whenever I do anything requiring intensive concentration for long periods of time, *I am conditioned to caffeine;* if you tried to take it away from me, you would see a violent side of my nature you probably never suspected existed! This is a crutch.

DEPENDENCY ON CRUTCHES INCREASES QUICKLY

Dependency on crutches—*and usually for increasing quantities of whatever the crutch consists of*—tends to grow very strong very quickly. In my case, I'm not talking about a *glass* of Diet Coke® beside me (that's how I started); I'm talking about a 2-liter bottle!

Alcohol is especially dangerous. Even for those who enjoy teleprospecting, it is a stressful undertaking. One drink at lunchtime to help you relax can far too quickly become two the next day, or possibly even one in the morning.

Never using a crutch is much easier to deal with than breaking free. The more you call *without* crutches, the stronger you become; *the less you will need anything extraneous to the process itself to help you.*

CRUTCHES OFTEN SUPPORT RESISTANCE

In addition, crutches often fortify your old enemy, *resistance.* Pouring another glass of soda, smoking another cigarette, all of these little activities are actually right up there with big excuses in that the bottom line is the same; *each delays your next call.*

BRIEF DELAYS TO PSYCH YOURSELF UP ARE NOT "CRUTCHES"

But *brief* delays to "get centered" more often than not are in an entirely different category. "Usually, before I begin," offers Mark Rubin, in Syracuse, New York, "I call *two or three* friends, or current clients, to get in the mode."

The key here is, two or three. If your inclination is to call more, be suspicious!

"When I hit too many rejections in a row," adds Randy Crawford, the Fort Collins, Colorado, salesman quoted earlier, "I get up and walk around, for a few minutes."

And I will admit, sometimes I spent a moment or so focusing on my "lucky crystal." I'm not convinced it ever actually got me any additional appointments, but I *felt* better holding it.

As with sympathetic magic, lucky objects can also hook into something timeless in the human psyche. If you believe it's absolute nonsense, forget it, but if you're not completely convinced one way or the other, you've got nothing to lose by selecting whatever (of reasonable size!) catches your imagination and bringing it with you.

However, far more is required. *Resistance* is not easily put to rest.

RESISTANCE—HOW IT OPERATES

Despite the rewards, teleprospecting is hard work, involving intensive concentration, heavy stress, hammering rejection, and at times suffocating monotony. Therefore, sometimes I resist; sometimes I would much rather be doing virtually anything else, a goal in which my subconscious fully supports me.

"ANYTHING ELSE" TAKES MANY FORMS

Anything else can take numerous forms; many *seem* deceptively noble. As with teleprospecting, writing can be rewarding but also emotionally draining. Therefore, sometimes I resist it. As I sit here now writing this, it occurs to me that it would only take a few minutes if I went to see whether my mail has arrived. It *could* contain something requiring immediate attention, and I have to stop anyway because if I don't water my plants at once, they'll never forgive me.

DEALING WITH TELEPROSPECTING RESISTANCE BY RECOGNIZING IT

For me, resistance was rarely an issue when I called from a client's office. Except for the soda, which periodically needed fresh ice, potential distractions there related to the client's life, not mine, but in calling (and writing!) at home, it's always present, even when below the surface.

Most of the time, I *deal with it by recognizing it.* Once I see what's going on, I can make a commitment to myself that I'm not going to allow it to interfere. I remind myself that if I were in some other location—a client's office, for example—everything else would be on hold. My mail would wait; my plants would survive.

STAY WITH IT!

So I write the first sentence or make the first phone call, and then stay with it. *As I stay with it, what I'm doing becomes easier; the resistance diminishes.*

SEE WHAT'S HAPPENING

If you are in your own office, resisting cold calling, it's essential that you see what's happening. Do you *really* have to go through your mail immediately—or water your plants? Or return phone calls—or fill out forms—or organize your files—or plan tomorrow's agenda? It's not that these things should not be done; the question is *when?* The answer can be anything that suits you, *as long as none of it interferes with the specific block of time you have set aside for teleprospecting.*

GIVING YOURSELF PERMISSION TO CONCENTRATE ON ONE PROJECT

Sometimes it also helps to remind myself that there are other blocks of time in my life when I do only one thing. When I spend two hours in a movie, I'm not also filing my fingernails. I carve out blocks of time for particular purposes; everything else goes on hold, and—so far, at least—the world has not ended.

REJECTION!

At last, you've made it through the initial resistance! You pick up the phone, you give it your very best shot.

Salesperson ... so, would next Thursday at one be good for you, or would you prefer Friday, at ten?

Prospect Listen, maggot, I know where you live. I know where your *mother* lives. If you ever call me again—

Now what?

"I'd hang up on them," says Mark Rubin, in Syracuse, New York. "I'd hang up first, because I'd feel better; more in control.

"People are either people, or they're garbage," he continues. "If they're garbage, it's their problem, not mine. Besides, given the statistics, the sooner you get off the line with someone like that, the closer you are to reaching a receptive prospect."

"If you get cold indifference," says Walt Worsham, the Augusta, Georgia, salesman, "it's hard to turn the crank on that prospect, anyway. But that's okay. You have to go through the forest to get to the trees you want."

Indeed, giving yourself permission simply to accept the "no's" is important.

"I think of what I made on my last sale to a cold-call prospect," adds Mark Rubin. "Then I divide it by the number of calls I made. This means each call averaged out to be worth X number of dollars. It means that regardless of individual results every time I picked up the phone, I made money."

In summary, turndowns are not "bad"; *they are simply part of the process.*

A SWIMMING POOL FULL OF MARBLES

Picture a swimming pool filled with colored marbles. When you call, you are sorting through the marbles—tossing them over your shoulder, out of the pool—in search of the solid white ones. These are the appointments which probably any reasonably competent teleprospector could collect. There are only a certain number of them. You can't change that number, nor can you find them without a *lot* of digging and tossing.

However, in with the marbles are also some that are solid gray. These, an *exceptional* telephone cold caller will bring in. There aren't nearly as many, *nor are they necessarily any better than the others,* but they *are* additional appointments.

Quite often—white or gray—luck is a factor. But *most* of the time, the issue is skill, defined as a combination of training and intuition.

WHEN TO SAY "WHEN"

How much time is the pursuit of any individual appointment worth?

In most cases, *not much.* Absolutely, the one you did not pursue with letters and calls and calls and letters may turn into someone else's prize sale for the year, *but if you put that same time into setting up four other appointments*, the *odds* are much more in your favor that you will *in total* sell more!

In summary, most of the calls you make *will* be "no's," but, assuming you've done your homework, *you have absolutely no control over this.*

Nor does it matter. As long as I know I have a good pitch, well presented, I *know* that a long dry spell means only that the next "hit" is right around the corner.

This is *very* important for me to remember!

REJECTION SYNDROME IS COMPLEX

Still, most of the insurance salespeople I've known over the years—even those who teleprospect very well—are not 100 percent comfortable with it, nor are the outsiders they hire. Although many factors come into play here, I believe the most powerful is the entire rejection syndrome, which is actually considerably more complex than has been suggested thus far.

UNDERSTANDING REJECTION

As human beings, at our most basic core of who we are, we want to be liked and respected, we *need* to be taken seriously. In *insurance* cold-calling, most of the time you will not only be rejected, but often those rejections will be insultingly personal.

IT'S NOT PERSONAL!

Yet, at the same time, they're *not* personal.

"You can't take it personally," says Shari Halloran, in Topeka, Kansas. "In the beginning, I did. I used to just die. But then I realized, they're going through whatever they're going through; it's *not* personal."

In addition, in *cold* calling, you are connecting with *complete* strangers. Just like the rest of us, those strangers have problems, sources of stress about which we know nothing, and now—on top of everything else—they have to deal with an irrelevant interruption.

In Vista, California, Rayda Roundy expands on this theme: "I never know what I've caught on the other end of the line. They could be busy, under all kinds of pressure. I didn't create whatever they're going through when they pick up the phone."

Additionally, most people would be happier if they had no need for insurance. Buying insurance requires an admission, to some degree, that none of us is invulnerable; it's a dimension of life none of us enjoys confronting.

And as if that weren't bad enough, insurance costs money. In the United States, where *85 percent of the population has no savings*—lives from paycheck to paycheck, often paying off credit cards as best they can from each of those paychecks—money is frequently a lot tighter than most people like to admit.

The irony is, although all of these are reasons *to* sit down seriously with an insurance salesperson, they are exactly the reasons why so many prospective clients resist.

RESPECTING THE SERVICE YOU ARE PERFORMING

It may also help to remember, when you make a cold-call appointment *you are performing a vital service*. The fact that the prospects have agreed to see you means they know perfectly well they *should* at least review what they have or need, but if you hadn't called, when—if at all—would they have done it?

"We're the good guys," says Shari Halloran, 'John Scott's business manager,' in Topeka, Kansas. "Get out of the business if you don't believe in what you're doing."

In Augusta, Georgia, Walt Worsham expands, "I don't think of myself as 'selling insurance.' I provide solutions to people's financial problems. We use insurance to fund people's objectives: income replacement, retirement. We protect their businesses. We pay their estate taxes.

"You know, when somebody dies, the hospital, the doctor, the lawyer—they all want to be paid. That's when the person nobody even wanted to talk to comes in to provide what the family needs most—*money*."

But you are to be credited not only because you *got their attention*. Even if they were already moving toward whatever they need, would they have gotten as good a deal as you'll give them—or would the follow-up service have been as responsible?

And often—as you already know—you really *can* save the client at least something.

"*See* you about my car insurance? What am I going to save?" a prospect asked Ed Lennon, of the Prudential Agency in Queens. "Fifty bucks? It's not worth it."

"Wow!" Ed answered. "It's not worth 15 minutes to save 50 bucks? You earn $200 an hour?"

He got the appointment.

And 50 bucks *is* a lot; *just ask anyone who needs it and doesn't have it!*

Remember St. George and the dragon? Hey, that's *you*—St. George! The dragon is the *prospect's* resistance!

PROSPECTS, ALSO, EMPLOY SALESPEOPLE!

Another point worth remembering occurred to me several years ago when I teleprospected someone in a neighboring state with an 800 number, who responded, "Okay. What's this about? I hope you're not using *my* WATTS line to sell me something."

I answered, "Sir, " I usually call someone "sir" if they seem to be looking for a fight. It's courteous, respectful *and acknowledges their power*, which more often than not is disarming. I'm not calling to fight; I'm calling to make an appointment.

"Sir, I assume your company employs salespeople. That does not suggest to me that your product is worthless. My product isn't worthless, either. Matter of fact, it's excellent, and something I think you'd find interesting."

He listened and then agreed to meet with my producer.

But this anecdote reflects a larger truth. *This country is a capitalistic economy; it is based on sales.* Even widget makers on factory lines are making those widgets to fit into a product which, eventually, *a salesperson will sell*. Therefore, everyone you speak to *needs salespeople*. When people you call are rude to you, it might help to remember that if others were consistently rude to *their* salespeople, pretty soon the person you're talking to would be out of a job!

GIVING YOURSELF PERMISSION TO INTERRUPT

All salespeople who cold call are interrupting the person they reach. That person was not expecting to spend time talking to a salesperson; they had something else to do with that time. We all know this before we even start dialing, which brings up another—usually less conscious—reason why teleprospectors are often uncomfortable with their work. As children, we're taught that it's rude to interrupt. Although we're no longer children, picking up the phone with the explicit intention of doing something we've been trained to believe is rude can still trigger all sorts of short circuits.

However, questioning assumptions formed in childhood is part of growing up. Reality is: interruptions are part of life. Commercials interrupt TV shows, stop lights interrupt traffic, illness interrupts vacation plans, and, every day, people who need other people's attention interrupt them to get it. *Particularly*, salespeople interrupt. If they didn't, many would never sell anything, and, consequently, the competition which keeps this country innovative would be substantially reduced. Granted, sometimes it is annoying (aren't you annoyed by it, sometimes?), but nobody ever died from it.

The bottom line is—salespeople interrupting potential customers to get their attention is a perfectly normal, necessary part of the overall economic process; it happens all the time. Assuming you are courteous and reasonable in your approach, if the person you're calling can't handle it, *they* have a problem—and it is a problem. In this as in any other business situation, to be rude is not only unnecessary, it's unprofessional.

MONEY: GOAL OR BY-PRODUCT?

Another primary reason teleprospectors—salespeople and outsiders—are frequently uncomfortable with the process is *money*.

When you focus on the money, you are not really with the person you're calling because you're not in the *now*; you're out there in an imaginary future, cashing imaginary checks.

It can also scare you. What if, you start thinking, you don't get any appointments? How are you going to pay your rent or your mortgage? When you fall into this mind-set, aside from the fact that it can stress you out, you can bank on it that the person you're talking to will know it. It may not be conscious, but they'll pick it up. Probably you'll push too hard; possibly you'll give up too soon, but whatever form it takes, people who otherwise might have agreed to see you will back off. Certainly we all need money, but you will teleprospect far more successfully if money is a by-product rather than a goal.

"YES, BUT WHO ARE YOU?"

It can also help to remember that teleprospecting is part of what you do; it's not who you *are*. Nor is the money you *have* who you *are*.

Years ago, a fledgling minister entered seminary school and soon realized the other students were playing a game with him.

"Who are you?" different groups repeatedly asked him.

"My name is—" he answered—repeatedly.

"Yes, but *who are you?*"

"Oh. Well, I'm a student here."

"Yes, but who are you?"

Finally, he realized it was a game—albeit a serious game—and gave it some serious thought. The next time the question arose, he ended the game by responding with a clarity he'd never really felt before, "I am a child of God and a happy man."

So—who are you? Whatever *your* answer, it can help to remember that you are *not* the sum total of your bank account in conjunction with the appointments you pulled in last week.

KEEP IT GREEN!

As mentioned earlier in this chapter, Mark Rubin in Syracuse, New York, calls friends or past clients to "warm up."

It can, indeed, help to "keep it green" by remembering past successes. You did it before; you can do it again.

PERMISSION TO HAVE FUN

One of the tools I found most helpful I initially thought was too offbeat to share. But when I started training others, I began to include it and promptly realized that what I was doing was as common as crabgrass, especially among both salespeople and outsiders who are exceptionally successful cold callers. Even outsiders poorly trained in virtually every other aspect of teleprospecting often did surprisingly well if they had this.

Again relating back to when we were children, virtually all of us were taught that work and play are separate. Do your home*work*, then you can *play*.

TELEPROSPECTING AS A GAME

But teleprospecting—serious as it is in reality—can also be one of the most interesting *games* you'll ever enjoy!

"If you put pressure on yourself to make every call work, you take the fun out of it," says Walt Worsham, in Augusta, Georgia.

This is a major resource; *if you can experience your cold calling as a game*, that playful kid who still exists in all of us can turn into a very serious ally!

I am an amateur artist; for me, some of the teleprospecting games I play include visual imagery.

"I use visualization," says Rayda Roundy, in Vista, California. "Actually, I use a lot of prepared motivational material." But *game* visualization is a specific subcategory, not to be confused with either "act as if" or the "sympathetic magic" visualization suggested earlier.

For you, *game* visualization may take an entirely different form, but as long as it takes *some* form, the *nature* of the stress you feel will probably change.

All stress is not necessarily negative. When properly channeled, initially negative stress can actually turn into the gasoline which keeps you going long after you'd expected to grind to a halt.

For me, after I've kicked off my shoes, taken about two slugs of my loaded-with-caffeine diet soda, made sure my pens actually write, and tended to all that other get-ready stuff, I sometimes bring up certain playful— even whimsical—images, *the more detailed, the better*! Sometimes I'm a large, sleek gray cat catching mice, which I'm going to take very good care of, or sometimes I'm about six years old wearing a white lace dress with pink trim and I'm on an Easter egg hunt. The appointments are the mice/the brightly colored eggs.

And then, of course, there's always chess!

But perhaps your taste runs more to football or video games. Or perhaps, for you, *imagery will have nothing to do with it.*

However, whatever your particular process may be, the bottom line remains the same: *give yourself permission to have fun*!

Many years ago, Sondra Watson, who now leads stress-reduction-through-humor workshops for a wide variety of client companies, worked as an insurance teleprospector.

"I was good at it," she says. "I got a lot of appointments. But I learned very early, you can't do it for money. Even though I needed the money, I never *felt* this while I was calling.

"If you like yourself and take it as a challenge—*a game*—to see how many you can get, it works," she continues. "My approach was very light. Most of the people I called were under such stress, such time pressure. A lot were grateful for the diversion. Sometimes we'd end up laughing together. If you can laugh with a person, it's much easier to build rapport. Often getting one appointment took a number of calls to the same person. Sometimes I wound up really liking them."

LIKING THE PEOPLE YOU CALL

Really liking them is also a tool, but one that may seem strange at first because in most cases, it means liking people before you've even made your initial contact with them.

For me, usually this was no problem simply because, in general, I like people.

However, occasionally I'm more specific, and you can be, also. One example comes immediately to mind. In one of my all-time most successful teleprospecting ventures, I called pharmacists only. Before I started—part of that get-ready stuff—I took a few minutes very consciously to remember pharmacists I'd known over the years who had been especially kind to me; the warmth I had felt toward them was very much in my mind as I dialed each number.

Or, in Fort Collins, Colorado, Randy Crawford specializes in working with older people. "I think of them as my grandparents," he says. "I loved my grandparents."

These *feelings* have a wonderful way of coming through and *reducing* other people's resistance.

In addition, they also bring you considerably closer to conveying what your call is really about: the emotional and economic security which only appropriate insurance coverage can offer.

READY, GET SET—

Now, you're ready! *Go for it!*

INDEX

timing and, 37-38, 133, 135-40
"Cold-call mailings", 159
Commercially prepared lists, 148-49, 151-55
Commissions, 110
Compensating independent teleprospectors, 105-14, 123
independents vs. scripted callers, 107
per appointment, 111-13
Competition, 38-39
Computers, 152, 179-80
Continuity, in hours and days, 117-18
Controllers, reaching, 150-51
Co-op insurance, 8
Corporate clients, 38
obtaining P&C X-dates from, 40
Correspondence, preapproach, 14, 51-52, 57, 58, 79
See also Mailings
Crandall, Charlotte, 114
Crawford, Randy, 42, 241, 253
Cross-category partnerships, 130-33, 213, 214
Crutches, dependency on, 239-40
Current event/insurance tie-ins, 51
Cyclical considerations, 133-34

D

Davidson, Bud, 110

Davis, Lynn, 203
Decision-makers, reaching, 79-80, 150-51
Door-opener categories, 43-53, 109
agency reputation, 49-50
current event tie-ins, 51
price/service advantage, 48-49
regional differences in personal style, 51-52
safety emphasis, 51
specialized expertise, 47-48
supermarket vs. boutique brokers, 46
surveys, 50
toll-free numbers, 46

E

Edwards, Suzanna, 46, 123, 201, 204-5
El Camino Insurance Agency, 65, 212
Employment considerations, 134-35
Expertise, specialized, 47-48
Expiration dates. *See* X-date

F

Fairbrother, Joni, 8, 77, 189, 200-201, 211
Financial institutions, and insurance telemarketing, 56
Five W's, and teleprospecting, 31-32
Flyers, 163